The Truth About SEO

Chris Lynch

Foreword

Josh Llewellyn-Jones

Editor

Louise Mumford

Foreword

I've never written a foreword in my life, however, when Chris asked me, I couldn't refuse - here's the reason why.

I met Chris Lynch many years ago and it wasn't long before I realised his knowledge for SEO and website development was second to none.

In today's digital world, there are many people trying to make quick money by offering poor advice or by using jargon that the typical business owner doesn't understand or, more importantly, doesn't want to understand.

What I love about this book is that not only will it help the one-man-band understand how to improve his website, it'll help the business owner when talking to the agency. It'll provide questions that agencies just don't expect.

This book is genius. I think it will make a great start of weeding out the chaff from the digital agency world and helping the business owner understand more, in a simpler form.

Josh Llewellyn-Jones
World Record Holder, Speaker & Brand Ambassador
Founder, J Squared Marketing

Introduction

What is SEO?

SEO stands for "Search Engine Optimization".

If you bought this book, you probably already know what that means - or at least you think you know what it means. If what you think it means is "How do I get my website to number 1 on Google?" then the very first thing that we need to do is realign your expectations of search engine optimization.

Sorry.

Today, any reputable SEO provider has long ago stopped promising to get you to "Number 1 on Google", to get you on the "front page", or really to get you anywhere specific at all. The SEO industry has laboured since its inception against a tsunami of bad practice, empty promises, and snake oil salesmen clicking the heels of their shiny shoes together and promising you that there's "gold in that thar' Internet". Even today, when you'd expect people to know better, I still receive emails daily that promise me an absolutely incredible, and also totally undeliverable, result from hiring a new SEO agency.

So, even if you're just reading the preview of this book on Amazon, then take this piece of advice with you - SEO companies who promise to get you to the front page of Google are not going to deliver what you're expecting.

There is only one **guaranteed way to appear on the front page of Google for a particular search phrase**, and that's to be the highest bidder. If you have deep enough pockets, you can be the top listing. The top organic, or "free", listing for any worthwhile phrase by comparison is volatile, transitory, and subject to the constant changing and improvement of Google's search engine algorithm.

But... there's hope.

Reputable SEO agencies will talk about improving traffic. They might generate more traffic for you, or they might look to reshape your traffic so that it is more appropriate for your website and brings you more enquiries/sales/followers etc. Sensible SEO measures from where you are and looks for improvement, as opposed to posting a flag on Google's green and promising to sink a hole in one.

The reality is that many, many websites are underperforming today - appearing lower in the search engine results than they should, or, in the worst cases, not appearing at all. Many businesses with a great product or great service are being let down by poor quality websites from agencies and providers who don't care about how well their clients do online, or who just don't understand the fundamental mechanics behind good website building.

There is also always the opportunity to be the new, disruptive, player in any niche or vertical market. People launch businesses every day on the Internet and, thanks to the egalitarian nature of most of Google's organic search requirements, they are fighting on a level(ish) playing field.

In this book, I'm going to teach how you can improve both the volume and the quality of your website traffic using free tools and without spending a penny on advertising. You'll do everything yourself, building an understanding of both your own website and Search Engine Optimisation along the way.

Ready? Good, let's go...

No, hold on, I've got some questions...

If this is SEO, what is SEM? Or UX? Or that other thing...

What about SEM? That's "Search Engine Marketing" and isn't that better for me than SEO?

Well, in my opinion, there's very little difference. You'll also hear people talk about Search Engine Marketing, Content Marketing, Social Marketing, Conversion Optimisation, and "UX" - short for "User eXperience" as if they are some sort of black art, a dark magic that only they truly understand. When they do this, they're not telling you the whole truth - today you might not understand what these things are, but you don't need to go to Hogwarts to change that.

All of the things in this list, ultimately, are just techniques aimed at doing one of two things:

1. Getting more people to your website.
2. Making the people on your website do something you want them to...

Oscar Wilde said that "there's nothing new under the sun" and that's certainly true of the Internet. There are no new things - just new ways to do the things we're already doing, just better.

So, when we talk about SEO in this book, we're really going to be talking about a whole range of processes and techniques that can:

1. Get more people onto your website.
2. Make the people on your website do something you want them to.

and some of these will certainly cross into the worlds of SEM, Content Marketing, Social Marketing, Conversion Optimisation, UX etc.

There's a very good reason that I called this an SEO book though - more people search for SEO than any of those other topics combined.

That's lesson one right there - find out what words and phrases your potential customers are searching for, and make sure you use the same language.

Nah, I'm good. I don't think I need SEO...

Before we get into the main part of the book... I'm going to get something off my chest. I've honest-to-goodness heard people say "Oh, I don't do SEO" like that's something to be proud of.

Here's maybe the most important tip in this book... it's not something to be proud of.

In today's 100% digital world saying that you "don't do SEO" is the equivalent of saying "Oh, I leave my business completely to chance" or "Oh, I let my competitors steal my business all the time".

It's ridiculous.

Now, if you're one of these people you probably aren't even reading this book but... just in case... I'm going to give you a get out of jail free card.

SEO is changing.

In fact, it's changing so much, so often, that that sentence is probably the only one that I won't rewrite in the next edition of this book. And there will be a next edition, there *has* to be, because...

SEO is changing.

When I sat down to write this book, I didn't want to use the phrase SEO because, in truth, optimising your website is about far more than optimising it for organic search. It's about improving the user's experience. It's about making sure you provide a great online service, tightly integrated with a great offline service. It's about protecting customers data. It's about speed, reliability, compatibility, and accessibility.

It's about every aspect of your business becoming digital and supporting your digital strategy - which, as the world is now completely digital should just be called "your strategy".

But... that's a lot to get on the cover of a book and most people, rightly or wrongly, still call this stuff "SEO".

So, here it is, my "SEO Book" and lesson one is this - **you need to do SEO.**

Isn't SEO dead?

Wait a minute. I read the Internet. The Internet says "SEO is dead!"

Yes, I've heard it too but, like Samuel Clements, the rumours of SEO's death have been greatly exaggerated. What *is* dead is SEO as we once knew it. The days of looking for technical "tricks" to work around the search engines algorithms are over and the days of any sort of automated content generation, magical link building, or SEO-by-posting-comments-on-other-people's-blogs are seriously numbered (probably to minus 1 day and falling).

There's a simple reason for this, and it's Google's own "**Web Spam**" team.

Google has invested a huge amount of time and money in building a team dedicated not only to improving its index, but also in protecting it. They are on a crusade to ensure that their search engine remains the first choice for any Internet user and their primary enemy is anyone who is trying to position a site in a better position than the one it "deserves" according to their algorithm. If you're an SEO provider, sometimes that means you're Google's enemy, whether you meant to be or not. But, let's face it, if your brand has been accepted into the Oxford English Dictionary as the verb for searching the Internet, you'd want to make sure you protected your investment too, wouldn't you?

Under the auspices of the web spam team, Google has released multiple significant updates to its index including the famously codenamed Panda, Penguin, Hummingbird, and more. The ramifications of some of these are still being felt by businesses today. Google is also still updating, and adding more update projects to its schedule. Tracking Google updates has become a daily task for webmasters and SEO consultants, with whole web communities dedicated to analyzing and discussing what Google may, or may not, be doing.

It's easy to see why people would be proclaiming that SEO is "dead".

Obviously, I don't agree, or I wouldn't be writing a book about SEO today. Throughout this book though, I've been careful to stay away from any tool, tip, or technique that I believe may fall foul of a Google update any time in the future. Am I psychic? No, sadly not, but I do have a few very simple rules that I believe can guide you in understanding which tactics are likely to be viewed as "spam" by Google in the future.

The Rules of SEO

RULE 1: If you can automate it, it's probably SPAM

Google believes in a "human-generated" internet. Any content, link, or page generated by a machine alone is likely to be classed as SPAM at some point in the future.

This also includes downloading content from another site or provider and regurgitating it on your own website. The days of cheap "affiliate" sites that could reproduce a manufacturer or supplier content but with generally better SEO are truly dead.

RULE 2: If you're doing it "because it's good for SEO" or "good for Google" but not "good for the user", it's probably SPAM

Anything done to a website purely to help it position better and that has zero benefit for the end user is probably a SPAM tactic. Whatever you do to your website, whether you do it under the banner of SEO or not, should be done to improve the experience for the user. Google wants to deliver its customers to websites that give them a great experience - if that's you, they will position you better.

RULE 3: If you are paying an unknown third party for something, it's probably SPAM

Anything that promises links, clicks, or traffic from undefined sources in exchange for money is either a straight out con or more SPAM (unless we're talking about a clearly paid for advertisement). Google doesn't have a problem with you buying advertising from them or from anyone else - but they don't like to see links, social media updates, or blog posts that are made to look organic but have really been bought and paid for.

RULE 4: If someone tells you it will "trick" or "trap" Google, it's probably SPAM

No matter who it is you are talking to, if they tell you they've figured out something Google doesn't know about its own system... then they're wrong (or soon will be). The problem with any SEO "trick" is that Google gets to hear about them pretty quickly. Any technique that works is invariably engineered out of the algorithm in very short order. At best, the benefits are real but transitory. At worst, those real benefits become real penalties if Google think you've been trying to abuse the system.

RULE 5: If someone told you about it in a SPAM email, it's probably SPAM.

The snake oil salesmen of yesterday still exist today and they're still shilling their wares via email, social media, and good old-fashioned cold calling. If a company is resorting to SPAM email to get your attention, how good do you think their SEO is really going to be? Shouldn't they be living handsomely off the customers who find their website organically?

Hit delete and move on.

White Hats, Black Hats, and Negative SEO

Before we continue, and on the topic of snake oil salesmen, I'm going to make a quick note here for you about the two kinds of SEO that you might hear talked about on the web - "White Hat" and "Black Hat".

They're nicknamed this way because, in a Western, the good guy normally wears a white hat and the bad guy wears a black hat. It's the same with SEO; the "White Hat" guys are trying to be "good" and play by the rules, whilst the "Black Hat" guys are out there trying to break the rules.

By now, I hope by now I've already warned you off the sort of tools and tactics that are ultimately only going to damage your website but, as one final warning, don't be fooled by self-proclaimed "Black Hat" SEO providers. In recent years, offering "Black Hat" SEO has become something that some providers specialize in. They want you to believe that their "Black Hat" techniques are going to go undetected by Google and that they are selling you something better than a "normal" SEO provider. The truth is, it's extremely unlikely that any "Black Hat" tactic is going to have a long shelf life. Google are watching these guys constantly and in the rare occasions that they do achieve something spectacular, Google have been known to dish out penalties manually to websites that it believes are breaking the rules.

Remember, Google is a business and a closed system. Whilst they are under increasing scrutiny from government bodies, there is no law that they have to rank your site, and they don't have to include it in their index. Their business is predicated on giving their users the "right" answer - not the answer that you want them to give.

Sadly, "Black Hat" tactics can not only be used by people on their own websites - but on other people's. A burgeoning area of endeavour for "Black Hat" SEOs is "Negative SEO". Negative SEO uses known "Black Hat" tactics, which carry known penalties, on a target website to try and attract a penalty from Google.

For example, if you're getting roundly trounced on Google's front page by your competitor around the corner, you might be tempted to hire a "Black Hat" to go off and do some of the things that I'm advising against doing but, instead of doing them to your website, they do them to your competitor. They don't need to hack the competitor's site to do this (although you will find that service offered on some darker corners of the Internet as well) as most negative SEO tends to be "off-site" - e.g. it is concerned with activities such as creating lots of SPAM links to a website that Google will perceive as being spam and therefore (potentially) issue a penalty for.

Google claim that Negative SEO is impossible but there are a growing number of case studies that show examples of it. I've seen it myself and whilst you might be able to debate how much real impact it can have, there is no doubt that it is going on.

Arghh... this is getting confusing! Can I really do my own SEO?

White Hats, Black Hats, Penguins, Pandas, Web Spam... it can all sound a bit daunting, right?

One of the things I'm most often asked by clients and colleagues is "How do you stay on top of all of this?" and the truth is that it takes a lot of time reading, experimenting, testing, and then reading some more to sort the wheat from the chaff. SEO best practice changes frequently and there is always something new to learn. What was true today may not be true tomorrow but, in this day and age, you can say that about a lot of things and even in SEO there are certain "evergreen" truths that seem unshakeable.

1. Don't spam.
2. Don't cheat.
3. Build a good website.

In short, you don't have to be a chef to make a good meal; you don't have to be a plumber to stop your sink leaking...and you don't have to be an SEO consultant to take control of your website and improve things.

DIY SEO is about understanding the fundamental, evergreen aspects of SEO that will pay dividends when applied properly. If, after that, you still want to hire an SEO consultant that's great - every penny you spend with them should be going into something worthwhile, not into fixing basic things that should never have been wrong in the first place.

Look, I'm really busy. I don't want to do my own SEO!

"Can't someone else do it?"
- Homer Simpson

There's nothing wrong with using an SEO agency, hiring an SEO specialist, and having someone else do all the legwork. SEO is hard, it takes **graft**, and you may not think you have the time. That's *fine*.

But I don't think you want to risk giving someone else, inside or outside your business, control of something so fundamental without having an understanding of it.

If you've ever sat in a meeting and not understood a word of what that person responsible for your website is saying, if you've ever thought "that doesn't sound right" but not known what questions to ask, if you've ever stared at a graph or a report and realised that you didn't know if it meant things were getting better or worse, if you've ever had that nagging dread that you're handing money over to someone and not getting a return on it... this is the book for you.

Francis Bacon was right when he said "knowledge is power": you don't have to be doing the day-to-day SEO work to understand how it works, what doesn't work, what should be happening and how to measure it.

No matter what business I might be in, I'd be damned if I didn't make sure I *understood* that part of my business. I'd be damned if I didn't understand every part. A long time ago, I worked in retail and before you could run a store you had to work in *every* department. You had to know how *every* part of the business worked. Looking back, that was a very sensible thing for them to do.

Make no mistake - you need to KNOW this, even if you don't DO this.

That's the preamble over. Still ready? OK, now let's go!

The One Thing That Matters and the Four Things You Can Do About It

The One Thing That Matters: ROI

If I asked what you wanted to get out of reading this book, what would say?

The answer, I guess, would be "a successful website", or maybe a "*more* successful website". But... what does that mean? What does **success** actually look like?

Do you want more traffic? Do you want people to spend more time on your site? Do you want to be higher up the search engine rankings?

All good ideas. But also... all wrong.

I've worked with lots of different companies on lots of different projects. At the start of the project, there will be a huge number of competing priorities, a plethora of "must have" features, and dictats coming in left, right, and centre. The website *is* the business, so everyone wants to have a say.

That is, of course, **before the site goes live**.

Once the site is live, there is one metric and one metric only that people then want to talk about - **return on investment**.

Return on investment is measured in pounds, or dollars, or euros. It's the simple measure of how much the site generates minus how much money the site costs to run.

Ben Hunt-Davies asked, "Will it make the boat go faster?" I like to ask, "Will that sell more boats?"

To get a return on investment we need **measurable conversions** - points at which the "visitor" becomes a "customer" and we can put a value to it.

You need to work out what your conversion point is - it might be a sale, it might be the completion of a sign-up form, or downloading a file. Whatever it is, the only true metric of whether or the not the website "works" is the total value generated by visitors reaching these goals and being converted.

All other metrics are steps before or after this point, either contributing to or being a consequence of this one crucial point. I've seen clients debate for days the shade of blue on a page, never once asking what shade of blue is most likely to get a customer to buy something (I know the answer to this, but I will take that secret to my grave).

That same client was banging the door of the office down, figuratively speaking, six months after launch wanting to talk about increasing website sales.

Like I say, once the site is live *everyone gets a lot more focused on what really matters.*

Smart projects, and smart website developers, **tie everything back to the ROI** from day one.

If you didn't do this, it doesn't matter - what's important is that you do this as of **now** and you keep your focus on this indefinitely. The only measure of success for your SEO project is Return on Investment.

But wait, my SEO consultant is telling me that metric X is more important than conversions right now.

They're lying, fire them.

The Four Things You Can Do About Value & Return on Investment

Just as ROI is calculated as how much value the site generates minus the costs of running the site, there is also a simple equation for working out how much value the site generates, and it has just **three variables**.

Visits x Conversion Rate x Conversion Value = Value

So, if I get 100 website visitors a day, and I convert 2% of them at an average order value of £20 I get...

100 x 2% x £20 = £40

The fourth thing you can do is to reduce **costs**.

There are acquisition costs from cost per click marketing, social media advertising, organic SEO consultancy, and the costs of reasonably priced books on SEO that will transform your life forever (like this one).

There are conversion costs in terms of offering discounts and incentives and for payment processing with payment providers.

There are costs that directly reduce conversion value as well: costs of products, cost of shipping, handling, etc.

So, if I get 100 website visitors a day, and I convert 2% of them at an average order value of £20, *and I spent £5 on marketing and the products cost me £2 each I get...*

*(100 x 2% x £20) - £5 -£2 - £2 = **£31***

You want a more successful website? It comes down to four things:

1. Increase the number of visitors to your website.
2. Increase the percentage of customers who convert.
3. Increase the value of the conversion.
4. Reduce the costs associated with each step.

The Jurassic Park Test

"Your scientists were so preoccupied with whether or not they could, they didn't stop to think if they should."
- Dr. Ian Malcolm, Jurassic Park

Anything you do to your website, anything at all, should be aimed at achieving at least one of these four aims. If you don't know why you're about do something to your website and how you are going to measure how effective that thing is, here's a simple piece of advice:

Don't do it.

The fifth reason to do something

There is **one** other good reason to do something to your website and it's actually the one that could have the biggest impact on the calculation… system risk.

Let's assume the numbers we used in the past example are for just one day. Let's also assume that every other day goes just like the one before and we live for a year in some strange, Groundhog Day world where each day brings the same sales as the day before.

Where do we end up?

$$((100 \times 2\% \times £20) - £5 - (2 \times £2)) \times 365 = \textbf{£11,315}$$

Now let's imagine that, actually, our website is down 10% of the time. If we're lucky, that only costs us 10% of the sales.

$$((100 \times 2\% \times £20) - £5 - (2 \times £2)) \times 365 = \textbf{£11,315 - 10\%} = £10,183.50$$

You're only going to get a Return on Investment from a website that is up and running. Eliminating or mitigating technical system risk is vital to protecting your ROI, as is ensuring that your website is compliant with all legal requirements.

*(And, yes... I know you've "saved" the money you would have spent on advertising and you still have the product, but I'm not interested in the cash we already have and the stock in the warehouse. We want to generate **sales** - that's the lifeblood of the business. Inventory doesn't sit there silently, storing product costs money too.)*

It may not be as glamorous as "making the boat go faster", but keeping the boat afloat is important. Nobody wants to be the fastest boat on the ocean floor.

Dungeons and Dragons

The internet is full of strange and arcane terms for fairly boring, mundane things.

Don't be fooled - we are all just nerds trying to make our jobs sound cool. Sometimes the marketing guys get in on it too - IT is a great industry for taking something you've always had, or bringing back something you used to have and we took away, and giving it a new name so that we can sell it to you again.

Here are some of the most important terms you're going to find in this book, and what they really mean.

"HTML": HyperText Markup Language. The code that web pages are made up from. You can see it if you use the "View Source" option in your web browser. Stuff like this: `<h1>Hello World</h1>` is hypertext.

"The Cloud": Somebody else's computer(s) that you access remotely.

"Spider": A piece of software reads a web page, follows the links on it, and then reads the pages it finds. Spiders "crawl" the web.

"Link Juice": When one website links to another, it passes "value" to the site - the internet's equivalent of a vote. Back around 2007, a chap called Greg Boser decided to call this value "Link Juice". I think it sounds kind of gross, but lots of people talk about Link Juice so... there you are.

"No Follow Link": People concerned about losing their "link juice" love "no follow" links. A no-follow link contains a special, hidden code that tells the spider not to go down that path. A no-follow link passes no link juice.

"Robot": See Spider.

"ROI": Return on Investment - how much money you make as a consequence of the money you put in. Measuring the return on investment that your website provides is crucial - if you don't measure this, then your website may just be a vanity project.

"D(a)emon": An unattended process. The "mail daemon" does not rule over the special part of hell reserved for delivery people who think it is OK to leave your parcel in your bin and not even put a note through the door - it just sends and receives mail.

"Server": Might be an unattended process or might be a physical or virtual device. (So, the "web server" might be a physical or virtual device which is separate from the "database server", or we might be talking about two bits of software which are both running on the same real or virtual device).

"Network Marketer": Someone selling to friends and contacts via their online social network. In many instances, also the new name for someone running a pyramid scheme. If Charles Ponzi were alive today he would probably be a "network marketer".

"Vertical Market": In short - what you do and who you do it for. Search engines don't cope with websites that address multiple needs very well, so a lot of SEO advice will focus on working within your "vertical".

"Virtual Server": A portion of a larger physical server that acts like a real server. Typically a virtual server can easily be resized to provide more, or less, resources as and when required.

The ABCs of SEO

A + B + C = ?

Google says that there are thousands of different "ranking factors" that affect where your website appears in their index.

I believe that all of these ranking factors can be broken down into one of three broad categories:

- Architecture
- Backlinking
- Content

Within each of these categories is a cornucopia of different factors and your total SEO score is based on how well you score against these factors in each of the three categories.

Put simply: **A+B+C = SEO**

Google emphasise and de-emphasise different factors, and different categories, at different times.

There was a time when an architectural problem, e.g. a technical problem with the build of your website, was sufficient to remove you from the index completely. There are still a few problems like this, but overall Google and the other search engines have become much better at working around technical issues in website construction. That's not a reason to ignore technical issues, but if you focus *only* on these issues then you'll be missing two-thirds of the picture.

Backlinks (links from other websites to yours) were, without doubt, the most important factor for a very long time. Google reputedly experimented with an index that did not take backlinks into account and it failed to produce good results. Backlinks are notoriously easy to manipulate, sadly, and so Google and the other search engines have increasingly stringent rules on what kind of links they consider "good" and which "bad".

Today, the mantra of many an SEO is "Content is King". Google's most recent update (Medic) focusses very much on the quality of your content, how much of an "expert" you appear to be, how much authority you have in your sphere/niche/sector, and how trustworthy your website appears.

As each factor increases or decreases in relative importance, the true SEO equation therefore begins to expand:

(A x Importance of A) + (B x Importance of B) + (C x Importance of C) = SEO

Focussing on only one area is risky.

Create great content, but on a flawed website with no backlinks? No traffic.

Great website construction, but poor content and no backlinks? No traffic.

Great content and a great website but no backlinks... well, that's a more interesting story. Google's approach to backlinking is that every backlink should be organic, earned by your website purely by it having a great design, brilliant content, etc. In reality, your first few backlinks are going to have to come from *somewhere*.

The internet is not Kevin Costner's baseball stadium from "Field of Dreams". Just because you build it, doesn't mean that they will come.

We'll talk about this more in the section on backlinking below.

For now, just remember - ticking all three boxes is the safest option when trying to improve your website.

A is for Architecture

What do you mean by "architecture"?

When we talk about website architecture, we're talking about the fundamental technology and construction of the website, the tools used to build it and the way in which it has been configured on the technical level.

Arguably, I could have just called this "Technology", but that doesn't start with A!

Picking the technology (or architecture!) to run your site

If you're serious about SEO, then you will want your website to have a Content Management System (CMS) under the hood. Without this, you're going to have a hard time updating your own content, and being able to add and update content to your website is essential - **never leave yourself in a situation where you need to ask a third party to do this for you.**

There are *lots* of content management systems out there and new ones are created with surprising regularity. Given that more than 99% of what happens on the internet is people downloading and reading/watching/listening to something, you'd think that we'd have nailed down this technology by now but, like a lot of things, exactly which CMS is right for you is going to depend on your own requirements and tastes.

For that reason, I'm not going to recommend a CMS, but I will give you a list of minimum features that any CMS that is serious about SEO will include. Check this list against your current website and, if you're thinking of building a new website, make sure your CMS can handle these requirements.

A note on Wordpress

You can't say "CMS" without someone bringing up Wordpress.

In what may be the most controversial paragraph of this book I'm going to say this…

I don't like Wordpress. It's bloated, slow, has constant security problems, the plugin and themes system is a mess of incompatibility and "pay to play" crippleware, and too many people deploy it without fully understanding what is required to maintain it.

If I was just 1% more of a nerd than I am, I'd get that on a t-shirt. And I'm a big nerd.

The SEO ABC CMS checklist

Here are the things that your CMS absolutely **must** do:

1. Allow you to change page titles and descriptions.

2. Allow you to change and control URLs for pages.

3. Give you a WYSIWYG editor.

4. Give you control over menus.

5. Handle image uploading and resizing.

6. Handle embedding media, such as YouTube videos

7. Allow you to add redirects for missing or replaced pages.

8. Allow you to categorise, tag, and organise content

9. Allow you to create your own forms (such as contact forms)

10. Easily share your content to social media channels

The SEO ABC website MOT

Assuming you already have a website, and that you want to improve the SEO of that website **without** rebuilding it, there are some standard tests you should apply to make sure that everything is as it should be. Without a solid architectural foundation, even the best-written website in the world will struggle to achieve a high ranking.

I'm going to walk you through a website architecture MOT *now*.

Clean or "Human Readable" URLs

Your URLs (the addresses for the pages of your website) should be as "clean" as possible and human readable.

What does this mean? Let's take a look at an example:

Dirty URL: https://www.mywebsite.com/?page=25

Clean URL: https://www.mywebsite.com/contact

The dirty URL contains URL parameters - everything after (and including) the question mark. The clean URL does not contain these things. The clean URL also gives the user a much clearer idea of what they are going to get when they click the link.

A URL is not clean if it contains a question mark.

Clean URLs can, and should, contain keywords relevant to the page - more on that later. It's also important to keep URLs as short as possible. Not only do some search engines prefer shorter URLs but the shorter and simpler a URL is, the easier it is to give to somebody over the phone, fit on a business card, type correctly into an email, or fit on the side of a bus.

A customer should be able to tell what the content of a page is going to be **just** from the URL.

If you can't imagine a BBC World Service presenter reading out your URL for the attention of an ageing dowager, then it's probably not a clean URL.

It's not always possible to keep every single URL perfectly clean. If you're running an eCommerce site, for example, your CMS is unlikely to produce a perfectly clean URL for every possible combination of filters a customer might choose on a product search page. There are also certain actions, like a customer search, where parameters may need to be passed to the site that are dynamic and therefore can't be cleaned in advance.

The important thing is to make sure that the URLs of your **landing pages**, by which I mean all the pages that you want people to be able to land on by clicking-through from a search engine result, are clean. If the user interacts with the page and the URL picks up some parameters after that, that's completely fine.

Meta titles and meta descriptions

Optimising your meta titles and meta descriptions is **absolutely crucial for SEO**.

Whilst you can't see your metadata when you're looking at your website, it's probably the first thing that a new customer sees *before they see your website*. Why? Because Google uses your Meta Title and Meta Description data to build the link to, and description of, your site when you appear on a search engine results page.

Having good metadata not only affects how well you rank but also affects how likely a user is to click on your link (which in turn then affects how you rank in future so... this is pretty important stuff!)

I'll cover the detail of how best to construct these in the Content section below but, for now, your job is to check two things:

1. Check that your website is outputting a meta title and meta description in its HTML.
2. Check that you know how to change the meta title and meta description against each page and post in your CMS.

A good CMS will include reports that can tell you which pages have had their metadata set up and which do not.

My advice is to **never** leave metadata to chance. Don't trust your CMS to build it for you - make sure you've handcrafted your meta titles and meta descriptions.

It's also important to eliminate duplication in your meta titles and meta descriptions as well - so check if your CMS has tools available that can check for duplicate.

Use of headings in your website theme

If you're using a CMS then the layout of your pages will be controlled by the skin or "theme" that is installed as part of your site.

Embedded in this theme will be headings. In HTML (the code that tells your web browser what your web page should look like) headings have a particular set of "tags" associated with them, running hierarchically from Heading 1 (H1) down to Heading 6 (H6).

A page should therefore be structured as follows:

- Main Title = Heading 1
  - First Sub-Headings = Heading 2
  - Next Sub-Headings = Heading 2
    - First Sub-Sub-Heading = Heading 3

and so on and so forth. Headings should be nested logically and should describe the structure of your document.

When a search engine looks at a page and doesn't find headings, we are leaving it without a map to understand the content on the page. Equally, where it finds a confusing or inconsistent use of headings, this can also be a problem.

There's a big difference between

- H1
    - H2
    - H2
        - H3
        - H3
            - H4
        - H3
    - H2

And

- H1
- H3
- H2
- H4
- H4
- H4
- H2

Even for a human being, the first structure is far easier to understand and work with than the second.

Sadly, there are a lot of themes out there that misuse headings not to convey the structure of the document but as a shortcut to controlling formatting. Heading 1 (H1) is normally big and bold, H2 is a little smaller, etc. etc. By using headings incorrectly, theme developers are passing search engines incorrect information about the structure of data and content on the page.

A well-written theme will not use heading tags to control style, but will use them to explain the structure of the information on the page.

Here are some things you can check by looking at the HTML for your web pages:

1. Look at the HTML for your pages (find out how in the "How To" section).
2. Press Ctrl+F to search your HTML.
3. Check how many times <h1> or <H1> exists.
4. Check for <h2>, <H2>, <h3>, <H3> etc. the same way, note where they are used and whether these are genuine "headings" or not.

If you do find that there's a problem with the way headings are being used on your web pages, you'll need to speak to your website developer to have them fixed.

Should I use my keywords in my headings?

Absolutely, of course you should - as long as they belong there.

If your page is genuinely about the "Size 5 Widget" then you should naturally put "Size 5 Widget" in at least one heading - preferably H1, near the top of the page.

You don't need to stuff headings with keywords - search engines understand that these pieces of text are important and weight the text contained within them accordingly.

Can I have more than one H1?

In the examples above I've only used a single H1 (Heading 1) tag.

For quite some time, the rule has been to only ever have **one** H1 tag on a page. With the advent of HTML5, an update to the HTML standard, we have seen the introduction of "semantic" tags - tags that do not affect the layout of the page but help web browsers and search engine spiders to understand what different pieces of a webpage do.

There are tags, for example, that are wrapped around the site navigation/menus and the site footer, isolating these from the main body of the content. The content, equally, can be divided into articles and sections.

If you are using HTML5 and have properly broken up your page into these semantic elements, each element can have its own independent H1 tag.

If "Semantic Elements" means as much to you as "Satanic Elephants" then keep it simple and insist on one H1 tag per page.

Image alt tags

When you add an image to a page on your website, you can also add an "alt" property to the image. Many people call this the "alt tag". This alt-property explains, in plain text, what the image is a picture of.

This is great for accessibility, especially for visitors who use a screen reader or other assistive technology (see below). It's also a good opportunity to slip some extra keywords into the page. A word of warning however - some unscrupulous SEO types will tell you to push lots of keywords into these alt-properties and over-stuff them.

Bad idea.

What your users want is a clear, concise description of the image, and this is what the search engines will be looking for too. Don't be tempted by the Dark Side.

Check robots.txt

robots.txt is a small, plain text file that's a part of your website. Its job is to tell the search engine spiders (those bits of software that crawl the web and index your site) what parts of your website they are, and aren't, allowed look at.

If you're using a Content Management System (CMS) like Wordpress, Typo3, Concrete5, or any of the others on the market there will be parts of your website's structure that the CMS does not want the spiders to go.

So far, so good... but what happens if your web developer (or you) make a mistake?

One of the most destructive errors I've seen is when a developer sets the robots.txt on a test site to a mode called "no-index". This effectively tells the search engines not to crawl the site or add it to the index.

Then, the site goes live... and nobody remembers to change robots.txt.

To the "naked eye" looking at your website through a normal browser, you will have no idea that anything is wrong. But, to a search engine, your site just became effectively invisible. Worse, if you *were* already indexed, you just told the search engine to remove you from the index.

You can check your robots.txt using **Google Search Console** or ask your web developer to verify that everything is as it should be.

Remember that a robots.txt issue need not be sitewide - you may find pages or sections of your website that are blocked whilst others are fine.

Check your XML sitemap

An XML sitemap is a computer-generated map of your website (in eXtensible Markup Language) that tells search engines about every page on your website. As well as telling the search engines where it is, your XML sitemap can also tell the search engines how important a page is and when it was last updated.

So, do you need one?

Search engines, particularly Google, won't index content that they cannot reach by navigating to it from your homepage. It doesn't need to be linked directly *from* your homepage, but if you can't trace a route of clicks from your homepage to a particular page, then it is unlikely to appear in the index.

But that's not the important thing about an XML sitemap...

The important thing about an XML sitemap is that you can use it with tools like Google's own "Search Console" to check that your website is being indexed.

If you point Search Console at your site's XML sitemap then you can get a measure of how many pages from the list contained in the sitemap are being actually indexed.

This is a great way to spot indexation problems like orphaned pages - pages that have become disconnected from the main navigation and are therefore not being indexed anymore.

Check, or ask your web developer to check, the following things:

1.   Check your CMS is generating a sitemap.

2. Check there is metadata in your page header to tell search engines where to find your XML sitemap.
3. Check your XML sitemap is connected to Search Console.

www vs non-www. subdomains

Do you know the difference between a domain and a sub-domain?

mysite.com is a domain. **www.mysite.com** is actually a *subdomain.*

It's the www. that makes all the difference. Chances are you also have a mail.mysite.com, maybe an ftp.mysite.com, and possibly many others.

Typically the www. subdomain is the default because, well, humans are lazy and we don't always bother to type www. at the start of a web address.

From an SEO perspective however, being able to see the same site at mysite.com and www.mysite.com is a problem because these two different subdomains can be indexed separately by search engines.

I have my doubts about whether or not Google really see a big issue here - they're smart enough, surely, to pick up on the fact that www. and non-www. sites are the same but, equally, why take the risk?

If nothing else, making sure that your website redirects one of these two options to the other so that your website either *always* has www. as the subdomain, or *never* has it, will give those pesky SEO consultants one fewer thing to ~~moan about~~ comment on.

This redirect is being configured directly on your web server. If you can load both www. and non-www. versions of your website in your browser, make sure your developer updates your server settings accordingly.

No page should be more than 3 clicks from the homepage

OK, this one straddles the line between Architecture and Content somewhat, but I've got it here because if your site structure is complicated or broken then it may take some help from your web developer to fix.

Every page on your website should be within three clicks of the homepage. **Maximum**.

Why? Firstly, users are pretty lazy (yes, you!) and we've been ~~spoilt~~ trained by search engines to expect instant, fast answers to questions. So, if I land on your website you've got a very small opportunity to get me from where I *land* to where you want me to be. Remember, everything we do has to either:

1. Get people to our website.
2. Get people on our website to do the thing we want them to do.

So, we don't put our products all the way at the back of the shop and make people walk a long way to get them. Instead, we put our best, freshest, most colourful products at the front of the shop to entice the customer to make that first step (or click). We keep the distance between arrival and goal as short as possible.

There's a reason supermarkets have flowers and fruit and veg at the front and the men's underpants near the back...

"Ah, this is a fresh shop! Everything here is fresh! I shall do well here" - Eddie Izzard

The second reason for keeping pages close to the homepage is the decreasing value of pages as they move further from the home page. I've managed to write almost 11K words on SEO without having to use the phrase I hate most in the SEO industry... **Link Juice**, but here we go...

You might remember "Link Juice" from our Dungeons and Dragons list of web terminology, but here's a more complete definition:

Link "Juice" is the magically, ethereal "something" that one page passes to another when it links to it. So, if page X is worth 100 Juice and links to page Y, page Y gets a portion of that "Juice" passed to it. Page Y links to Page Z but it has less juice than X, so passes on a smaller amount again to Z.

When someone links to your website from theirs, more often than not they will link to your homepage. Your homepage therefore collects a *lot* of Juice (at least, hopefully it does). Pages just one step away from the homepage are therefore viewed as important, pages two steps away less important, and so on and so forth.

Rich snippets provide additional data about your site to search engines and can improve your SEO and result output

Websites are complicated and whilst search engine boffins are pretty clever, even they need a little help now and then to work out just what a web page is all about.

This is where rich snippets come in.

(My editor thinks "Rich Snippets" would make a great band name. If this whole SEO thing ever falls through, I'm starting up a jazz five-piece called "Chris Lynch and the Rich Snippets")

Rich snippets are another invisible form of metadata that is embedded into the code of your webpage to provide search engines with extra information about what is on the page.

There are meta-data descriptions for products, events, even recipes. Make sure you check if there is a meta-data type compatible with your website content and, if there is, **use it**.

Make your site secure

You can tell the difference between a secure and an insecure site by the presence (or not!) of a padlock next to the URL in your browser. When you see the padlock it means that the data that you are exchanging with the website is being encrypted. Sites that have been through a process called "Enhanced Verification" or "EV" have had their real-world credentials checked and will present a green background on the URL/address bar to show their credentials.

We've had secure sites for a long time and the technology is essential in protecting credit card and other personal data as it moves across the web.

Google has been pushing something they call "HTTPS Everywhere" for quite a while too - the idea that every site (not page!) should use encryption at all times.

So keen are Google on this that they've been very open in stating that they've made it a "ranking signal" - something that directly affects your search engine ranking. So - even if you're not collecting personal data, there's a good reason to get your site secured right there.

It's also an incredibly cheap thing to do - Google, Facebook, and others have been funding projects like www.letsencrypt.org, which issues completely free security certificates, for some time.

The process to set up a new certificate takes around fifteen minutes tops for a developer or system administrator - so there's really no excuse for not getting this done as a matter of urgency if you currently don't have it.

Getting a padlock does not mean your site is secure

Let's be clear - just because a website has a padlock, even if it comes on a fancy green background, doesn't mean that it is "secure". All it means is that data you are exchanging with the website is secured whilst it is in transit across the internet. What happens to it once it *arrives* at the website is a whole different story.

It's like posting a letter in a very secure envelope. It's safe between the postbox and the destination, but once the envelope is removed the information is vulnerable again.

I've picked on Wordpress a few times already but it is one of the worst culprits for unfixed security problems - 268 are listed on cvedetails.com as I write this.

Two. Hundred. And. Sixty. Eight.

https://www.cvedetails.com/vulnerability-list/vendor_id-2337/product_id-4096/

And that's just the core code - it doesn't take into account plugins and themes that you may also be using on your website.

When pages go missing - the world of 301s and 404s

Over time, your website will change. You'll add pages and you'll take pages away. You will move pages and you will restructure. You may even rebuild, changing out your CMS for something new and better (and hopefully not Wordpress).

And that's a problem for search engines.

Search indexes maintain a list of all the pages that they've ever seen - that is, of course, effectively what the index is - a massive list of pages and information on what they contain that people then search.

As a consequence, search engines are rather touchy about the topic of pages going "missing" - probably because this reflects on them more than it does on you.

Imagine opening up an old-fashioned telephone directory, looking for a plumber and, when you call, finding that the number in the directory is out of date.

You're not going to blame the plumber, are you?

The SEO implications of missing pages

When a web page can't be found, your web server returns what is called a "404 error". Google Search Console records the number of 404 errors your site has; e.g. the number of pages that have gone missing; and this is believed to be a key metric in terms of search engine optimisation - the lower the better.

Even if Google weren't counting up your missing pages, there's another good reason to redirect missing pages, and that's to pass on the benefits of any links or general SEO "goodness" that page had accrued on to its successor.

Imagine you had spent a year building backlinks to pages all through your website. Then, you get a CMS upgrade and your URLs change. All of those backlinks are pointing to pages that don't exist and therefore have little (or probably absolutely no) value. Your site may just be about to tank.

The UX implications of missing pages

SEO aside, a 404 error is still something you should deal with - why would you leave a visitor to your website sitting on an error page when they could be looking at your product, your story, and engaging with your brand?

What to do about missing pages

Here are the things you should be doing to deal with missing pages.

1. Use 301 redirects

If you change the URL or a page, make sure you create a 301 redirect pointing to the new version of that page, or a replacement, to preserve SEO value and avoid losing customers.

If you don't know how to do this on your current website/CMS then learn - as quickly as humanly possible. It's vital that you are able to do this.

You will often need to create multiple redirects at once, so check to see if there is an option to import multiple redirects at once as well. It's not vital that you can do this, but it will save you a lot of time if you can.

2. Use 301 redirects properly

Don't redirect everything that you can't find to your homepage. It's lazy and Google will record it as a "soft 404". If you genuinely don't have a replacement for a page that's gone walkabout either create one or …

3. Learn how to fail gracefully

404 pages are like noses - most people have one and most people wouldn't pick theirs if anyone else was watching.

Joking apart, the 404 page is the "last chance saloon" of retaining a visitor to your website. You've *already* let them down - the thing they wanted is no longer there - the more gracefully, and *usefully*, you can do this the better.

"This isn't flying - this is falling with style"
- Buzz Lightyear

Good 404 pages have even become a category in web design all of their own, with their own awards and frequent "Top 10 404 Pages" blog articles popping up across the internet.

If you're stuck for inspiration, here are some things you can try on your 404 page to make it a little less… useless.

Give it personality and make it your own

Make sure your 404 page actually carries your branding - there are sites out there that either use the default 404 page for the CMS or the web server that they are hosted on. Disgraceful.

At the very least, say sorry that your visitor isn't able to find the page that they wanted. It's not an **error** - you've dropped the ball.

Give the user a chance to find what they wanted

Your 404 page should be topped and tailed with your normal site navigation.

Think about including latest or top selling products, most popular blog posts, and prominent links to pages where visitors can contact you, engage on social media, and find any terms and conditions or policy pages that site contains.

Over and above that, offering the customer a search option is a great way of keeping them on your website rather than sending them running back to wherever they came from.

Remember that the user has been there

A good CMS will keep its own record of 404 errors, giving you a chance to create a redirect before the search engines have the chance to notice that there is a problem.

The simplest place to do this is on the 404 page itself - make sure yours either records missed opportunities or passes this information on to your analytics platform (*more on those later!*)

Migrating URLs to avoid 404s

At the start of this section, I said that one of the events that can generate a lot of 404 errors is a change of CMS or website construction.

I wrote this down because it happens, not because it **has** to happen.

If you're changing your CMS and your URLs are already *clean, keyword rich (this is discussed in the Content section)* and *indexed* - do not change them.

Take it from someone who has used nearly every CMS available and has written more than three of his own. There is no good technical reason that you can't copy your URLs from one system to another.

I'm not saying that there's not *a* reason - you just won't convince me it's a **good** reason.

When Architecture Goes Bad

If you're going to put in the hours of toil, the pints of blood, and the gallons of tears required to create a great website, why on Earth would you accept it going offline?

Not only will your site's rankings be impacted if your site is regularly inaccessible, but you could be offline just when a customer needs you.

Ensuring that your website is running on fast, reliable, infrastructure is a must - but it's an area that a lot of website owners overlook, opting instead to go for the cheapest possible hosting they can find.

The first little pig ran his website on an out-of-date version of Wordpress hosted on a cheap shared server with no support contract, no SLA, and no backups.

Wolves ate him.

The number of business I've come across who are having problems with their websites simply because of bad infrastructure would amaze you. Although this is a technical topic, it's actually one of the easiest things to get right.

Here's are my tips for making sure that your infrastructure is giving your website the support it deserves:

Use a web host with good support

Problems happen and no technology, no hardware or software, is fault free.

"If General Motors had developed technology like Microsoft, we would all be driving cars that would crash twice a day for no reason whatsoever."
- General Motors Press Release

More than anything else, making sure that your hosting provider has a robust support process and a skilled team of system administrators and engineers is a must.

Of course, everyone will *tell you* that they have these things, so you're either going to have to dig around for information online or get a recommendation from somebody. Personally, I prefer a word-of-mouth recommendation from somebody that I trust over anonymous content on "trust" and "ratings" websites.

Status stalking

Most good hosting companies have a "status" page on their website that lets customers know if there are problems with any of their systems.

If the hosting company that you are looking at doesn't have one - bump them off the list. If they *do* have one - monitor it for a few days. Check to see if there are problems and, if there are, how quickly are they resolved? How good is the communication with customers when the problem is going on?

It's also worth looking at the hosting company's social media, in particular their Twitter feed; this is an easy way to find more historic information on problems that have occurred. Keep in mind that some savvy companies have a separate Twitter account for support and status announcements, so make sure you're looking at the right one if you're doing a little research.

Use a web host with reliable hardware and software

This should go without saying but... if you find that the host is having frequent problems (or worse, the same problem over and over again) when you're investigating their support arrangement - bump them off the list.

It may seem harsh, but if hosting is their business and they aren't doing it well, why should you let that affect your business? I can't think of a single logical reason why you would do that.

Beyond this, assessing how reliable a particular infrastructure is can be an extremely complex task. The biggest hosts, such as Amazon, offer such a plethora of hosting options and, whilst each has a solid underpinning from Amazon themselves, the way in which these are configured and connected together can have a huge impact on how reliable your website actually is.

In short - **working out if a particular *configuration* is reliable or not is a topic for a whole other book.**

If you're working with a web development agency then they may have a preferred hosting platform

Most web developers will have a relationship with a hosting provider and will either want to put you in touch with them or resell their services.

This is completely normal - but beware of a developer who sells "hosting" but won't tell you where they get it from. Either their markup is astronomical, they are selling you short in terms of capacity, they've got multiple customers packed on the same server like bees in a hive, or there's something else fishy about this arrangement. Find out who they use and then check them out.

Hosting is not an area to cut corners. The guys at Trotters Independent Hosting (Data Centres in New York, Paris, and Peckham) are not your friend.

Leave the cheap hosting to the bloggers - we need servers ready to do business.

Use a fast server

"I feel the need... the need for speed" - Maverick, Top Gun

Website speed matters. An increase in page load time of 1 sec can impact your conversion rates by up to 90%. People are lazy, in a hurry, and don't have time to wait for *your* website.

The quickest and easiest way to improve the performance of a website is to increase the specification of the hardware it is running on. More processing power, more memory, faster discs, and more (or faster) bandwidth are the order of the day - all of these things affect the speed at which your site will load.

However, they are *not* the whole story...

Most CMS platforms make poor use of resources. This is because, rather than your CMS being one "thing", it is actually a collection of "things", each thing made by a different person and none (or few) of them talking to each other.

Every time you add a "plugin" to a website you are adding **load** as well as **code.**

Configurations need to be loaded. Data needs to be picked up from the database. Data that has already been picked up might need to be altered or tweaked in some way. Other third-party components might need to be used... the list goes on.

A typical open source CMS with plugins and themes activated isn't a process that goes from "A" to "B" as rapidly as possible. It's more like a committee who insist on voting on everything between "A" and "B", including the manner in which the voting will take place, full terms of reference, and who spend half the meeting discussing nominations for treasurer every week. They do get to "B", but end up going via "F" because that was the consensus opinion at the time.

Of course, you can always add **more** plugins to help improve the speed of the site again - caching plugins, content delivery network plugins... the list goes on once more. A lot of these are great... just so long as they are compatible with each other, and all the other plugins you have, and the theme you have, and... the list goes on.

Why your website is slow today but wasn't last year (probably)

If your website seems to be slowing down, there are four areas to check: Scalability, Concurrency, RTSG, and KUWTJ.

Scalability

Scalability is the measure of how well a system copes when the size of things (except users) increases.

Imagine launching a website with 100 products on it. Now, jump forward in time and imagine your website is now selling over 10,000 products. Assuming the number of people on your website has remained the same, **scalability** is the measure of how well (or not) the website copes with having to search, sort, and display this increased volume of product.

Some eCommerce platforms are notoriously poor at scaling up to large product sets. If you are implementing a new site, check with your developer what the largest site in terms of the number of pieces of content or number of products they have handled is.

Fixing scalability problems is hard. You can overcome them by simply increasing your server capacity (we nerds call this "throwing iron at the problem") but this is a short-term fix. Long-term, you need to find the inefficiencies in the code and fix them, or move to a platform that can handle larger amounts of data.

Concurrency

Concurrency is the measure of how well a system copes when the number of parallel operations (or users) increases.

Imagine launching a website with 100 products on it, getting 100 visits a day, taking 2 orders. Now, jump forward in time and imagine that website still has 100 products on it, but now it is getting 1,000,000 visits a day and taking 20,000 orders.

See the difference? The size of the calculations didn't really change, but we have to do them far more often and do a lot of them at the same time.

Assuming you have a scalable system then concurrency is often just a matter of increasing parallel capacity in the system - "throw some iron" and get more/bigger servers. However, there can be bottlenecks - certain processes that cannot be parallelised or that have other capacity limitations on them. These problems are harder to fix.

The classic issue that impacts concurrency is database locking - multiple processes all wanting to update the same information (or type of information) in the database and creating an unscalable bottleneck as they all "lock" each other out whilst trying to "lock" the data they wanted to alter. Nasty.

RTGS

RTGS or "Rose Tinted Glasses Syndrome" is the psychological trick that our brains play on us to make us think everything used to be better than it is now. Yes, we can even get nostalgic about the websites and servers of yesteryear!

Joking aside, it's important to keep track of things like website loading times over the long term. "Thinking" something is running slower than it used to is not as compelling as "knowing" something is running slower because you've got proper analytics behind you.

KUWTJ

KUWTJ or "Keeping up with the Jones" is another trick we can play on ourselves.

Your website didn't *seem* slow a year ago, but it *seems* slow now. You check your analytics and the page load time is *exactly the same*... so what's going on? Whilst those well documented analytics have ensured you're are immunised against RTGS, what you might be noticing is not that your site got slow... **everyone else just got faster.**

Like sprinters who constantly chase shaving even 0.1 of a second off a World Record, the biggest players in the game know that every microsecond counts and are constantly looking to make their systems more scalable, more concurrent, and thus serve more things to more customers more often.

Loading testing in a nutshell

There are plenty of freely available loading testing applications out there that can test the speed of a website with simulated load/users and the right one depends on your chosen platform. No matter which way you go, technique is just as important as technology:

Here's a simple way to measure the concurrency of your website:

1. Run a load test - push your server to the point that errors occur to find its maximum capacity.
2. Double your server capacity.
3. Ensure that the server has been configured to use this   full   capacity.

(Some applications impose their own limits on how much resource they use.)

4. Run a load test - push your server to the point that errors occur to find its maximum capacity.

The resized server should be able to handle significantly more load than the original - assuming you have only a single server - then things like the operating system of the server won't take up *more* space on a larger server and so your "free capacity" should have more than doubled.

Here's a simple way to measure the scalability of your website:

1. Run a load test - push your server to the point that errors occur to find its maximum capacity.
2. Increase the size of your site with test or junk content.
   (Take a backup first, you want to be able to get back to where you were!)
3. Run a load test - push your server to the point that errors occur to find its maximum capacity.

The more data you pump into the system, the slower it will get. If you see no slow down at all you're either not adding enough stuff or your system has capacity to spare - keep going.

The point of a load test is not to pass - it's to fail under as much load as possible in the most graceful way possible. If your software didn't break, you didn't test it hard enough.

Why you should always ask for the specifications of your server, your CMS system requirements, and your website's capacity

Knowing the capacity of the server your site is hosted on and the requirements of the CMS might seem like something just for the techies, but it is really important at the management level as well.

Imagine coming up with the greatest marketing campaign of all time. It's perfection and you know it's going to bring 100x the normal traffic to your website. It launches 9AM on Saturday...

If you were running a bricks-and-mortar store you would put on extra staff, maybe get some of those velvet rope and brass pole things to manage the queues, and you'd get in early to make sure everything was ready.

Why wouldn't you do the same with your website?

Assuming that your website will cope with anything you throw at it is dangerous. Find out from your provider what the capacity of your server is and how much "headroom" you have. Headroom is the measure of how much unused capacity you have and lets you know how much extra load you can put on your website before there's a problem.

My web host says my hosting is elastic - what does this mean?

In an elastic environment, your server capacity should increase when your website is under increased load, adding additional capacity (normally in the form of additional servers) when they are needed. When things calm down, the size of your hosting springs back to normal - like elastic.

Elastic hosting is a great way to control hosting costs. You can't claw back unused processor time - if you commission a large server and it then sits idle, that's money down the drain. However, like anything technical - the more complicated it gets, the more moving parts there are, the more likely it is to break.

So, in an elastic hosting scenario, load testing is essential. You don't want your elastic to snap at the wrong moment, leaving your digital pants on the floor.

Your web host may say that they have already tested their elastic hosting environment. If so, insist on some documentation for the tests so you have an understanding of the amount of load that was involved.

Either that, or pull on the pants someone else has tested for you and assume they are OK...

On Reviews of Infrastructure and Platform

Today's exciting new technology that you simply must use is tomorrow's legacy platform that everyone winces when they talk about.

SEO is changing. Remember that? So is software. So is hosting infrastructure. The change is constant, relentless, and needs to be managed.

One of the things I hate most about the web development industry is the number of web developers who don't explain to their clients the need to maintain a website's software infrastructure after it's been implemented. There are far too many providers who simply install the latest version of "CMS X", configure it, apply a theme, and then walk away. Project complete. *Job done.*

And well it might be, but the job will be undone in a few weeks by the next security update or system patch that "CMS X" or one of the plugins are going to need.

This is why it is absolutely crucial that you have a **support contract** with whoever builds your website for you.

Your support should include:

1. Updates to the underlying server software - operating system, web server, database, etc.
2. Updates to the CMS software.
3. Updates to any plugins.
4. Updates to any themes.
5. Updates to any bespoke code that breaks down as a consequence of upgrades to 1, 2, 3, or 4 above.
6. Any queries.

It's reasonable to expect that your provider will want to be paid both for providing this support and for any work over and above what is agreed - you should note that *changes* to the website are not covered in the list above.

Backups!

If you lose your site then you lose your rankings, as search engines quickly remove sites that won't load and there's nothing worse for a customer than clicking a link that goes to a dead or broken website.

Make sure you have access to a recent backup of your website and make sure you download these backups and store them securely somewhere that you have access to.

If the worst happens and either your current web host or your website provider goes out of business, it could take weeks or even months to replicate all of the data in your website with a new provider.

My web developer says my site is Open Source, so I don't have to worry

They're lying; just because your website is open source, doesn't mean you don't need backups or that you shouldn't have access to them.

Nightmare scenario part 1: the jigsaw puzzle of death

Your website is made of CMS "X" extended by a bunch of additional components - plugins, themes, third-party plugins - all of which have been picked by your developer and all of which have their own particular version number. In addition to this, your developer may have written some code of their own, a bespoke theme (or tweaks to a bought-in design), changes to a plugin etc.

The way your website works is a product of that particular combination of components. Precisely that combination.

So, if your developer is planning on rebuilding your website in the event of a problem simply by downloading the same components - they haven't thought things through. What if the components or the CMS have changed? What if they aren't available anymore? And what about all those little tweaks and changes, probably undocumented, that the web developer made to get everything just so?

You'd have more chance of recreating George's Marvellous Medicine that you would have of recreating your website this way.

I'm a huge Open Source advocate, but just because something is Open Source does not mean it does not need to be maintained and properly looked after.

Nightmare scenario part 2: the empty CMS

While we're on this topic, let's also not forget that your **data and content** is not open source - that's all sitting in the database, *underneath* the CMS. It belongs to you and data is more valuable than gold.

So, if by some miracle your no-backups developer managers to reconstruct your website like CSI Miami at a crime scene, no backups still means that your data - blog posts, pages, products, even customers - it's all gone.

If you take nothing else away from this book, take this:

*Your business does not "have" data, your business **is** the data.*

My provider says that they are "Software as a Service"

This one is slightly more difficult. In this environment, you don't "own" the code for your website at all, all you have is a license to use a service for a specified amount of time.

Don't get me wrong - there are lots of great "Software as a Service" website platforms out there (I founded one of them!) and there are big advantages to working with a "Software as a Service" provider. It's simply a matter of understanding what you have and what you don't have.

If you are using a "Software as a Service" platform, here are the things you should ensure you will be able to access:

1. Access to **all** of your data - every page, post, customer, order, contact form submission... *everything*.
2. Access to **all** of your files - images, videos, logos, PDF attachments etc.

Make sure you understand how you can access this information. Ideally, you want to be able to download this information in bulk, not one item at a time, and you want to be able to download it in a format that will be easy to import to another system.

Never underestimate the power of the humble CSV file. It's the "spare gun in the ankle holster" of file formats. You might sneer at it, but one day it's going to save your digital backside.

CSV (Comma Separated Value) files are your friend - every spreadsheet application in the world can read them, every database can import them, and they are pretty much "human readable" if you want to open them in a text editor/word processor.

You should also make sure that your data is going to be somewhere safe if your "Software as a Service" provider goes to the wall. Often, when this happens (and it does happen often) the company gives customers a small window of opportunity to grab their data before the service shuts down for good.

Be prepared.

What you need to do, **today**

Every business needs to:

1. Ensure you have access to full data and file backups.

2. If you're working with an open source platform, ensure you can also access code backups.

3. If you're working with a proprietary platform or Software as a Service platform, ensure you have an agreement in place to gain access to source code in the event that the provider goes out of business.

4. Ensure you have documentation on how to restore backups to a fully working state.

5. Ensure you have tested the process in the documentation.

Brief notes on software "escrow"

When it comes to source code, providers who don't want to give you access to the code in the normal run of business may talk about a software "escrow" arrangement.

In effect, this means lodging a copy of the software with a trusted third party who will ensure it is released to you if the vendor is no longer able to provide the service and, for whatever reason, is not able to facilitate the transfer of the code themselves.

A perfectly good arrangement, just make sure you're working with a reliable escrow provider and that there is a documented and audited process in place for the software vendor to update the copy of the software that the escrow company is holding.

Closing The Architectural Toolbox

So, that was Architecture. Phew…

It may seem like a lot of technical grind (it was) and a lot of legal and contract stuff that wasn't as much as fun as you thought working on a website would be (again, it was). However, solid infrastructure is fundamental to growing any online business. Without it, all the backlinks and great content in the world won't amount to a thing.

The best content in the world is worthless on a broken website.

Or, to put it another way:

If you have to eat a frog, eat it first thing in the morning. If you have to eat two frogs, eat them both first thing in the morning and eat the big one first.

Get your infrastructure right. That's **eating the big one** first.

C is for Content

Whoa, hang on a minute... what happened to "B is for Backlinks"?

Well, as much as you can't have a good website without good Architecture, you can't build backlinks to content that doesn't exist. It's also much easier to build backlinks to content that is *good*, so we're going to start with building some *great* content and then we'll talk about getting links to it.

Content creation is one area where you can't "fake it 'til you make it". The "it" is the content... you've got to make it.

SEO is dead, long live content

If you've heard the phrase "SEO is dead" then you've probably also heard the phrase "content is king". *This* buzz-phrase, unlike the previous one, has some weight to it.

Google has been putting emphasis for some time on the quality of a website's content as the most important "ranking factor" in its index. This is a good thing - quality of content is certainly a more level playing field that the technical efficacy of a website or how many back-links it can garner.

It's also, for Google, an area where it is a lot harder to automatically generate a result. Focusing on content, rather than other areas, puts the focus back on the "human internet" and takes it away from things that can be manipulated by software or technical changes behind the scenes of a website that may be beyond some users to implement.

For website owners, creating quality is a good thing as well. Quality content gets readers, and it keeps them. Quality content helps convert readers into customers/subscribers/members etc. And quality content attracts that most elusive of things - the organic backlink.

So, quality content is an all-round good thing. **All we have to do now is understand what "quality" content really is...**

Thankfully, Google are rather more transparent in this area than in others.

How Google assesses the quality of content

We've talked a lot about Google's spiders and robots, but we haven't talked about its humans. It has lots of them.

Spread all over the globe, Google employs thousands of "Quality Assessors" who are employed to test the search index, look at the pages it returns as "top pages" for queries, and then manually rate them using a well-documented set of criteria.

Imagine what you could do for your website if you could get hold of one of those documents, right? You can. Just Google "Google Quality Assessor Guidelines".

It's one of the most overlooked, underrated, but absolutely essential things that anyone building and scaling websites should read, re-read, then read again with a batch of highlighters and sticky notes on hand.

Why hasn't your SEO guy put a copy of this document in your hands? Probably because he wants you to think that he trained at Hogwarts, interned with Gandalf the Grey, and might disappear back into The Matrix at any moment...

Either that, or he **doesn't know about it**.

Bottom line, if you haven't got a copy of this document then you need to go and get one. It may not live on *your* desk, but it should live on somebody's in your organisation - if only because it's pretty thick printed out and you can hit your web developer over the head with it.

(I don't actually condone violence to developers - we're a naturally skittish bunch and will retreat to our underground lairs if startled.)

Before you write another word - decide on your tone of voice

Musicians talk about finding "their sound". Writers often talk about finding "their voice". Even chefs will refer to a dish as "them on a plate", despite the fact that is actually quite a disgusting image when you think about.

Finding the "tone of voice" for your brand and then using it consistently across all of your communications and content is essential. Your tone of voice is the personality of your brand and it extends beyond just the written word - it should also be reflected in the design of your site, your use of imagery and any audio and video that you use.

Defining your tone of voice is not as nebulous and woolly a task as it might seem, thankfully - it can be done in just a few simple steps.

Step 1: Gather samples

Assuming that you already have content, gather samples of it. Cast a wide net - include web pages, emails, printed material, anything you can get your hands on.

Throw away anything where the content was provided by a third party - we only want content that is 100% constructed using the "raw DNA" of your brand.

Now, start to whittle down the content to those examples that you feel most represent your brand. For every piece of content ask "is this us?" and trust your gut instinct. A tone of voice is a *very* hard thing to force, so if it doesn't feel right then you shouldn't keep it. Go with what feels right and natural.

Step 1B: The Great (Brand) Escape

It's possible that, having whittled out everything that doesn't feel "right" you're left with little or nothing in your "me" pile. That's OK - it's just an indicator that, up to this point, you haven't been *authentic* in your communications and content.

It's not a problem, you just need to work out a new place to get some content. My recommendation is to replace your empty "me" pile with examples of content from brands that you love, aspire to, and would want to be like. Don't think in commercial terms - we're not all going to be Apple or Microsoft. Think in terms of whether, if Apple or Microsoft were at a party, would you want to talk to them - or would they be that guy you keep not-so-subtly moving to avoid being trapped in conversation with?

Step 1C: The sanity check

When you are repeating Step 1 above, it's worthwhile adding a nuance to your process to take into account that **not all change is for the better**.

When you have your pile of "keep" content and "throw away" content, *and not before*, grade each piece of content from 1 - 10 in terms of how effective it was.

If it was a piece of sales material, did it do a great job at generating sales interest? If it was a press release, did it get picked up by multiple outlets?

If you've got successful content in your "throw away" pile and duff content in your "keep" pile, you need to have a think about whether the evolution of your brand is for the better or not.

Don't do you if you suck.

Step 2: Make an idea board

Find a nice big wall or whiteboard you can work on and pin up your samples.

Take a big step back, take a deep breath, and **describe the brand you are looking at in three words**. Don't be afraid to get the whiteboard pens out, join some things together, write some random words up on the board, so on and so forth.

Coming up with new stuff like this is somewhat like testing if spaghetti is cooked - you're going to throw a lot of stuff at the wall, make a mess, and wait for something to stick.

The technical trick here is "**anthropomorphism**" - the attribution of human traits to an object (in this case, your brand/business).

Is it serious or fun? Traditional or unconventional? Compassionate or challenging?

Again, the important thing here is to be authentic. You might think you're the zany, crazy, new-kid-on-the-block but if you're not… you can't force it.

"Be yourself - everyone else is already taken" - Oscar Wilde

Once you have your three-word list, break each word down into three more words to better describe that attribute of your tone of voice.

For example, "Fun" might break down into "Comedic", "Irreverent" and "Cheeky".

Don't agonise over this breakdown, just make sure that you understand what each of your three traits means and that you iron out any ambiguity.

If you aren't a person, be a thing

If you're struggling to create a "human personality" for your brand (what are you, some kind of a monster?) then you can always fall back on the marketing stalwart of defining yourself in terms of other products/services.

If you were a car, a TV programme, a brand of yoghurt... take your pick. Personally, I prefer the personal approach but this technique has worked well for a lot of people.

Asking other people as well as asking yourself

Everyone is different and bringing in some trusted colleagues, friends, or advisors can be really helpful.

Marketers have been doing this for years - standing around in high streets with clipboards, asking people to taste two different brands of cola, etc.

Remember that **good** old fashioned market was good *before* it got old fashioned. Asking people what they think of a new brand *before* you launch it is much cheaper than looking at internet traffic and feedback on social media on your brand *after* you launched it and realising you got it wrong.

This is a lesson some brands have really learnt the hard way.

The Power of the Secret Ballot

Sometimes, people in your team/business won't want to tell you what they really think of your brand.

An anonymous survey or secret vote can help to surface opinions people might otherwise not be comfortable voicing.

Take everything you receive using this method with a pinch of salt however. If the Internet has taught us anything, it is that anonymity brings out the worst in many people.

Step 3: Do as I say by saying as I do

Now that you've carefully defined your authentic tone of voice, it's time to build some rules that will help to ensure that **every piece of content** you produce matches this tone.

It's as simple as creating a list of "Do" and "Don't" rules for content creation.

These are a checklist that we will check every piece of content against before it can be approved. Ideally, everything our brand says and does online and off will follow these guidelines as closely as possible.

Not every piece of content can tick every "do" - it's pretty hard to write a funny complaints procedure (by which I mean a procedure for handling complaints that is funny, not a procedure for handling funny complaints) - but no content should break a "don't".

Here's an example:

Trait	Description	Do	Don't
Fun: *Comedic,*	We're a brand	Engage in good	Lose sight of

Irreverent, and Cheeky	that knows how to have fun and doesn't take things too seriously.	natured banter. Poke fun at ourselves. Create things "just for fun". Share fun content from others.	our core audience. Stray into controversial or "edgy" content. Be cruel or sarcastic.
Traditional: *Trustworthy, Honest, Historic*	We still believe in old fashioned values.	Acknowledge our history. Share successes and failures. Tell the truth.	Mislead or trick readers. Oversell. Openly criticise competitors.
Compassionate: *Caring, Considerate, Socially Aware*	We're a brand that cares about our customers and the things that are important to them.	Own our mistakes - and explain how we fix them. Acknowledge how our actions make our customers feel - especially the good!	Make excuses. Ignore the impact of problems.

Now, you don't know anything about the brand I was describing here, but if I told you that I modelled this chart from a small toy maker - let's call them Geppetto Limited - I'm pretty confident you could write a tweet for them advertising their new puppet.

Here's one I made earlier:

Pinocchio - He's finally here, and you're going to love him. He's a chip off the old block...

In one tweet we:

- ☐ Tell the customer about the product.
- ☐ Include two emotive elements - the excitement that an anticipated product has arrived and the customer will love it.
- ☐ We've acknowledged our history - we've been working on this product for a while and... "he's a chip off the old block".
- ☐ Yes, that last part was our comedy. If you don't think that's funny then I simply can't help you.

We've ticked a "Do" against every aspect our voice and haven't broken any "Don't" rules - this content is good to go!

Step 4: Practice

Now that you have your list and your chart, you're ready to start updating and creating content so that it matches your tone of voice.

If you're working with a team, now is a great time to create exemplar content that they can use to further their understanding of the guidelines that you are giving them. We're not dealing with zeroes and ones here, so even with a detailed list of guidelines there will still be room for ambiguity and misinterpretation.

The clearer you can make things, the better.

"Ideas are easy. It's the execution of ideas that really separates the sheep from the goats" - Sue Grafton

From this point forward, the content guidelines are your laminated, framed, always-on-your-desk point of reference for every piece of content and communication you create.

At least... until you update them.

Step 5: Review and refine

At least once a quarter, you need to repeat the process outlined above.

Why? Because brands **change**.

It may be that your brand has evolved for commercial reasons (your business grew and had to become more "serious" to deal with new, bigger, more serious customers) or it may be human reasons (you have a new MD and he doesn't share your love of wood-based humour), or it could be something else - anything else at all! The point is that organisations, like organisms, don't stand still - they evolve.

So, every quarter you should repeat the process above to ensure that your guidelines still match your brand.

Before you write another word Part 2: Content strategy

Having decided the tone in which we are going to write the content for our website, we now have to decide what to write. We already know that we need to be writing expertly, with authority. We also know that search engines, just like humans, are looking for useful and timely content. We know we can't just rip that off from someone else... so where do we start?

It's back to the whiteboard folks, for a good old-fashioned brainstorming and planning session... *with a few technological twists.*

Climbing your website tree

Picture your website as an tree. The base of the trunk is the homepage, every page after that a branch, every other a smaller branch off one of the big branches, etc. If you draw this upside down, you've got what we call a "sitemap".

I don't like drawing the tree upside down because it makes it look too easy to get a user from the top to the bottom, as if gravity will naturally draw them down through your content when the exact opposite is true - **you have to earn every click**.

Imagine your customer, arriving at the base of your tree, has to climb their way **up** to the content that they want. Every branch takes effort to reach and the further they have to climb, the tougher and more tiring it gets.

The attention span of a web user is notoriously short. Depending on which article you decide to believe, the longest is around 12 seconds and the shortest around 5 seconds. It might not seem like you're asking a lot of a customer when you ask them to click from one page to another, but you are. (We'll talk about this in more detail in "The 5 Second Test" a bit later!)

The good news is that not every customer will need to climb the tree from the bottom. It is possible for a customer to land on any page of your website that they can find from a search engine or click to via a link. Great news... except that when this happens, gravity **does** take over - if the page they hit isn't right for them, there's a good chance they're going to fall off the tree - either back to the homepage or off your site completely.

What does all this mean? It means you shouldn't approach creating content without a *plan*. A plan that maps out your page from the homepage onwards (and upwards) and that identifies the purpose of every single page.

By "purpose" I mean that, for any page, you should be able to define its title, give a short description of it, and define what unique search phrase you are targeting with this piece of content.

If you can't write down the title, description, and search phrase for a page then you are not ready to write that page.

Drilling down: my technique for climbing website trees

Understanding how a website tree should be built doesn't make it any easier to build one, of course. Here's a technique that I've used to build structures with clients in the past that produces great results.

I ask questions.

OK, it's not *quite* that simple, but fundamentally that's what it boils down to. The trick is in the questions that I ask. A lot of consultants/developers/marketers will sit with their client and ask questions a bit like this:

Consultant: "What pages do you want on your website?"
Customer: "We need a homepage, a page about our team, a page about our products..."

This technique produces a horrible outcome for everyone because it requires the wrong people to do the wrong job. Why on Earth would your customer know what pages you need on a website - that's what the resident web expert is there to work out (or, at least, they should be).

A savvy customer answers the question like this:

Consultant: "What pages do you want on your website?"
Customer: "The ones that will get us the most customers and the most revenue. Let us know what they are."

Now, if you're from the consultant/developer/marketer camp you might be screaming right now: "How the hell am I supposed to know the answer to that?"

Here's a technique that I've used in the past to answer that question that produces great results.

I ask questions.

Here's how you do it...

1. Forget what you know

Forget anything you already know about your own business. Because you're going to be taking on the role of a brand new customer. Brand new to your product, brand new to your brand, brand new even to the concept of what you *do*.

2. Write down what you want to know

So, now that you've cleared your mind more effectively than a one-hundred-year-old Zen master, it's time to start asking questions. Imagine it like an interview process - you're still the new and sceptical customer and you need to be **convinced** of everything.

Here's an example I've worked through for a telecommunication company.

Website: Hi! I'm Brand X.

Customer: OK. What do you do?

Website: We sell IP Telephony.

Customer: What's IP Telephony?

Website: IP Telephony lets you make calls over the internet.

Customer: Why would I want to do that?

Website: It makes all calls cheaper, especially international calls.

Customer: OK, I like saving money. How much does it cost?

Website: There are a few different plans, it depends on call volume.

Customer: I never heard of you guys before, can I trust you?

Website: We've got a great team here and we've worked with big clients.

Customer: Sounds good, how do I get started?

Website: Just fill in this form…

Don't you wish all sales meetings were as easy as that?

It may seem a little weird to have this conversation, but you've got to accept that the most fundamental job your website has to do is **convert visitors to customers**. That might mean giving you their money, it might mean joining your mailing list, it might mean filling in a contact form. It doesn't matter what form it takes - the important point is that every page supports this process.

If you don't know why a particular page is on your website, what do you expect a customer to make of it?

3. Find the pages that answer the customer's questions

So, looking at the transcript above, how many pages can you see for this website?

I can see 6:

1. The homepage.
2. A page that explains what IP Telephony is.
3. A page that explains the benefits of IP Telephony.
4. A page that explains pricing.
5. A page about the company and who it has worked with.
6. A contact form.

It's not a lot, but you'd be amazed at the number of businesses that do very well online with little more than this.

Let's put these pages into a table now and start working on some of our titles and descriptions:

Page	Title	Description	Keywords
1	Save money on telephone calls with IP Telephony from Brand X.	Brand X are the IP Telephony providers who can save you money on your telephone calls.	...
2	What is IP Telephony and how does it work?	...	...
3	What are the benefits of IP Telephony?	...	...
4	How much does IP Telephony cost?	...	...
5	Who are Brand X and who have we worked with?	...	...
6	Contact Brand X about IP Telephony.	...	...

4. Rinse and Repeat

That's just one sequence of questions of course; to get the full value from this process you need to keep asking questions, keeping asking questions, and keep asking questions. Remember that getting a customer to contact you is a *conversion* - a win! The vast majority of customers will abandon your website if they can't find the information that they need without contacting you.

Here are some of the questions we didn't ask yet:

- ☐ Do I need a computer to use an IP phone?
- ☐ Do I need a fast broadband connection to use an IP phone?
- ☐ What is the call quality like?
- ☐ What happens if my broadband goes down?
- ☐ What happens if Brand X's systems go down?
- ☐ Can I switch my IP Telephones from Brand Z to Brand X?

A lot people bury the answers to these really important questions in a "Frequently Asked Questions" page. My advice is to take your FAQ page outside, lightly douse it in petrol, and set fire to it. It's a conversion killer and it's an SEO horror show.

A lot of people think that adding something to their FAQ page is solving a problem - but if a question is getting asked frequently by customers, doesn't it deserve its own webpage?

Worse than the super-long word-soup FAQ page are FAQs hidden behind an on-site search engine. There's nothing wrong with having an on-site search engine, but hiding pages so that the search is the only way to find them means you've lost any chance of them appearing on Google or any other search engine.

It was their job to answer a customer's question and get them to convert - you just locked them in the cupboard under the stairs like Harry Potter. You wouldn't do it to an employee, don't do it to a webpage.

Web pages **are** like employees in many ways - categorising like this is how you can understand the Five Types of Webpage and how to master them.

The Five Types of Webpage

There are five types of web page and you can map them to functions in your business to get a better understanding of what they do.

1. Signpost/Front of House
2. Marketing
3. Sales
4. Customer Services
5. Admin and Legal

Each type of page needs to be handled slightly differently to be effective.

The signpost page

The signpost page has one job - get the customer to where they need to be and do not let them leave.

Your homepage is your important signpost page. It has to mix marketing, sales, customer services, and some admin/legal work all into one layout. It's your "front of house" - the first time a new customer interacts with your brand, and it's got a lot of work to do.

The most important thing for a signpost page to do is to engage the customer and direct them clearly to where they need to go next.

Marketing

The job of a marketing page is to answer questions and provide information that will encourage the customer to convert (to "buy") **and** to give them a clear signpost on how they do that - linking to a product, product range, enquiry form, etc.

This type of page doesn't explicitly ask the customer for the conversion.

Sales

This page **does** explicitly ask the customer for the conversion. This is the type of page that has "Add to Cart" and a price on it, in case you're wondering.

Just like in the real world, marketing creates the opportunity and sales close it.

A sales page has two jobs:

1. Get the customer to take the next step.
2. If they *can't* or *won't* take that step - offer alternatives. Do not lose them.

If you're building an eCommerce site, everything from that "add to cart" page through to the basket and checkout process is a sales page.

Google has a special term for these type of pages in its quality guidelines - "Your Money or Your Life", and it really is that serious when it comes to eCommerce.

It's cost you a lot of time and money to get the customer to the stage where they have a product in their basket... don't screw it up now!

Customer services

A customer services page is unlikely to generate any revenue for you. Its job is the opposite - it is there to **save** you money by keeping customers happy and reducing the time spent on dealing with queries, problems and complaints.

This is the type of page where good old FAQs raise their head again. If you're selling a product that requires any degree of after-sales service, the more information you can provide on your website and the more "self-service" opportunities you can provide to your customer the better.

Customers like solving their own problems - in the modern, digital world making contact is the last resort for most consumers. Why do think that when people **do** want to make contact with a brand they increasingly do it on social media?

Between 2014 and 2015, complaints that were voiced on social media **increased eight-fold**. It's 2018 now and 60% of consumers say they would happily "call a brand out" on social media with a complaint.

The customer service page is there to keep complaints, queries, and other customer issues at bay by providing answers, self-service solutions, and a route for contact that doesn't involve screaming at the top of your digital lungs for the entire planet to hear on Twitter.

Never undervalue the importance of these pages - they can make a massive difference, not only to your return on investment in the short term, but also they go a long way to increasing the lifetime value of customers by keeping them happy and devoted to your brand.

"The best customer service is if the customer doesn't need to call you, doesn't need to talk to you. It just works."
- Jeff Bezos, Founder of Amazon

Admin & legal: The pages you have to have, even though nobody asks for them

This is the last type of page and the one that's most unlikely to come up in the question and answer session. You'll know it when you see it - it's those pages that every website has in its footer and that nobody ever reads:

- Terms and Conditions
- Privacy Policy
- Cookie Policy (sometimes inside Privacy Policy)
- Customer Service Policy

Some "Policy Pages" are a legal requirement and what you will need to have will differ with both your industry and with the geographic territory you are working in.

Other policy pages are there to cover you in the event that a customer has a problem with your goods or services - it's not uncommon for eCommerce sites to require customers to tick a box to say they "Agree to Terms and Conditions", even though they probably haven't read them.

In 2017, Jonathan Obar of York University in Toronto and Anne Oeldorf-Hirsch of the University of Connecticut ran an experiment using a fictional social network called "NameDrop". In the experiment, hundreds of college students tapped the big green "Join" button to become members of NameDrop. **But** according to paragraph 2.3.1 of the terms of service, they'd agreed to give NameDrop their future first-born children.

Only a quarter of the 543 students even bothered to look at the fine print. But "look" is not "read": on average, these more careful joiners spent around a minute with the thousands of words that make up NameDrop's privacy and service agreements. And then they all agreed to them.

So, putting your Terms and Conditions and Policies on your website might be a legal essential, but don't expect customers to pay attention to them!

Applying the five types to our content grid

Applying the five types to our content grid, we've now got something like this:

Page	Title	Description	Keywords	Type
1	Save money on telephone calls with IP Telephony from Brand X.	Brand X are the IP Telephony provider who can save you money on your telephone calls.	...	Signpost
2	What is IP Telephony and how does it work?	...	...	Marketing
3	What are the benefits of IP Telephony?	...	...	Marketing
4	How much does IP Telephony cost?	...	...	Sales
5	Who are Brand X and who have we worked with?	...	...	Marketing
6	Contact Brand X about IP Telephony.	...	...	Sales
7	Help and Support.	...	...	Customer Services
8	Terms and Conditions.	...	...	Admin & Legal

You'll note that I've classified "How much does IP Telephony Cost" as a Sales page rather than a Marketing page. This comes back to the very first bit of sales training I ever received, working on a shop floor of a UK retailer - **reading buying signs.**

If someone walks in holding their cheque-book, it's a crime to let them leave without writing a cheque.

What about blog posts and news?

These get a job, but they don't live on the tree.

Why? Because blog posts and news are transitory - the older they get the further down the blog they will be pushed (assuming you keep blogging, which you absolutely must do!) and whilst we will revisit *pages* on our website to revise and improve them it's not necessary to do this with blog posts.

If there is new news on a topic or something changes - write a **new** blog post.

And, in case you can't guess - blog posts are *sales* pages.

If you're blogging about a product - link to it. If you're blogging about a service - link to it. Failing anything else, ask the reader to contact you for more information. A blog post without a call to action is a sad thing indeed.

Building titles and descriptions using keywords

Our grid still isn't complete though - we need to write our page descriptions and decide on what keywords/search phrases we are targeting for each one.

This is where we apply our technical twist and use some simple online tools to understand the language that our customer is using and what they are looking for.

Why titles and descriptions matter

Page titles and page descriptions (what we call "Meta Titles" and "Meta Descriptions" in the business) are hugely important. Not only do these two pieces of data have a significant impact on your search engine position as a "ranking factor", but they are also the first things that a customer will see from you **before** they reach your website.

Most of us will search the internet every day for something. We type our search into Google and we get back a list of results. We decide which we click based on what Google shows us - the title and the description of the page, positioned as Google sees fit. It's the great leveller of search - your fancy design is invisible right now and you're competing with everyone else using just two bits of data.

Thinking about your click-through rate from Google (the percentage of people who see your site **and** click on it rather than someone else) is pretty sobering.

Imagine standing in your brand new, fully kitted out shop, full of the latest products and the best prices... and watching customers walk past you and into your competitor. That's what a low   rate is - and it sucks.

In the movie business, they call it an "elevator pitch" - a pitch delivered in the time it takes for an elevator ride. Those movie guys are lucky - they might get a couple of minutes. On the web, your elevator pitch has a matter of seconds to hit the mark.

So, how do we build titles and descriptions that draw customers in and how do we create titles and descriptions that will rank so customers even see them? Read on...

Title and description keyword building tips

Search engines rank pages - make sure each page on your site has a purpose and a distinct keyword strategy.

First and foremost, each and every page needs a unique keyword/search phrase.

This **does not** mean that you can't use the same words - our IP Telephony site would be pretty poor if we only mentioned IP Telephony on one page - but you should have a unique title and description for each page and therefore a unique search phrase you are targeting.

As we've already learnt - if you don't know what a page is for, how is the customer ever going to know?

What you do need to do is identify your **base search term** - the thing that your website is fundamentally about. In the example we've been using, our base term would be "IP Telephony". This should be an easy thing to spot (hopefully!) - it's fundamentally what your business/website is about.

Embrace the "long tail"

Part of getting unique search phrases for each page is embracing what is called "the long tail".

A long-tail search is a keyword phrase that contains at least three words. They're more specific and often less competitive than generic keyword terms.

Since the dawn of time (at least in internet terms) we've got better at searching the internet. The internet has gotten a heck of a lot bigger too. Today more than 40% of searches are four or more words.

In short - people ask more specific questions and so we can have far more specific targeting of pages.

"Fast is fine, but accuracy is everything"
- Xenophon

But, how are we going to achieve this accuracy if we don't know what the customer is looking for. We can't see their searches, can we?

Or... can we?

How we did it in the old days...

In the "old days", Google used to tell you in your analytics what search terms somebody had used before they came to your site. Google doesn't do that anymore and many an SEO laments the passing of this "golden age".

Personally, I don't care. Knowing what people who came to your website searched for is interesting, especially if we look at where they then went and what they did. However, knowing what people who do **and don't** come to your website are searching for is far more interesting.

"The purpose of a business is to create a customer"
- Peter Drucker

It's essential that you research your keywords before you optimise for them.

And if your SEO guy is telling you that you can't find out what people search for... he's lying.

How to use Google to find popular searches

Just like your phone, Google tries to predict what you're going to type before you have to type it. It does this using the combined search history not just of your account, but of many others.

This means that you can go to Google and find out what other people are searching for. Here's how you do it:

1. Go to the right Google for your region.
2. Type in your base search term ("IP Telephony").
3. Type in the letter "a".
4. Watch the drop down - you're seeing the most popular searches that began with "IP Telephony a".
5. Make a note of any interesting search terms.
6. Go back to step 3 with the next letter of the alphabet.

Using the process I found some of the usual suspects and also surprises like:

1. "IP Telephony bandwidth" - (How good a network do I need?)
2. "IP Telephony encryption".
3. "IP Telephony free".

Work through the process for "a" through to "z" at least.

You can also try this technique using parts of sentences, questions in particular work well:

- "Why does *IP Telephony*..." (a-z)
- "What does *IP Telephony*..." (a-z)
- "When does *IP Telephony*..." (a-z)
- "How does *IP Telephony*..." (a-z)
- "Can *IP Telephony*..." (a-z)
- "Does *IP Telephony*..." (a-z)

And, a particular favourite of mine:

⬜ "IP Telephony vs …"

It's also worth doing this with your own brand name and the brand name of your competitors. Whilst optimising for your competitors' brands isn't an advisable tactic, looking at what questions people have about them should inform you what sort of questions people might have about you.

A-Z profiling can also be extended to use multiple letters: "IP Telephony aa" followed by "IP Telephony ab" etc. etc. This is pretty time consuming but can turn up some results. I've seen software marketed that automates this process but be advised - Google is pretty good at spotting automated searching and will temporarily block you if it thinks you're misbehaving.

Overall, I find this a great way to plug gaps in a keyword strategy and to make sure we're answering all of the customer's questions - not just the ones we thought of. It's also a useful way to make sure you're "tuned in" to the customer and speaking *their* language…

Speaking your customer's language

One of the great things about spending some time "searching in your own neighbourhood" like this is that you're going to be speaking *their language*. People say that the best way to get to know a foreign language is to immerse yourself in it, and that is exactly what you will be doing.

Many industries, hobbies, and businesses have their own internal language - but that doesn't mean that your customers know it. David Ogilvy said, "Our business is infested with idiots who try to impress by using pretentious jargon." No matter what business you're in, I'm guessing you'd agree that that is true.

Communication requires commonality of language. Dump the jargon and speak to the customer in words they understand.

Thinking about intent

One last piece of advice when it comes to using this technique - think about the customer's **intent,** e.g. think about not only *what* they are looking for when they search, but *why* they are looking for it.

I'd much rather rank my site number one for "Best place to buy IP Telephony" than for "IP Telephony Problems", wouldn't you? (Unless your whole business was fixing problems!)

Search engines make a lot of effort to try and interpret the customer's intent when running a search and this is one of the reasons why there are sometimes shopping results and sometimes not, why there are sometimes videos and sometimes not, etc. etc.

In a little while you're going to hear about a turtle, a gatepost, and the "Five Second Rule" - keep intent in mind when you're reading that. If you misread the customer's intent, you **will** fail the Five Second Rule test.

How to use Google Ads to research keywords

Before we leave keyword planning behind there is one more useful tool I'd like to introduce you to: **Google Ads**.

Now, don't panic - we're not going to pay a single penny/cent to Google for what we're about to do, but you *are* going to need a Google Ads account. You can sign up, completely for free, at https://ads.google.com

Once you've signed up and logged in, check in the "Tools" menu for something called the "Keyword Planner". Inside Keyword Planner you can do a few really interesting things like:

- Get recommendations from Google for keywords based on a phrase, word, or even the content of your website.
- See historic traffic and forecasted future traffic for a keyword or phrase.

What's really interesting in this data is that Google gives you, in bandings at least, the number of searches for your terms *and* tells you how hotly those terms are contested for advertising spend. I find it logical to assume to that if there's high competition for adverts, there will be high competition for organic position as well.

The holy grail, of course, is a keyword with Low Competition and a large number of searches. Unless you are in a very narrow niche, you'll be exceptionally lucky to find one of those unless you exploit *The Long Tail* and start working through 4+ word searches.

Don't try to target keywords that are not relevant for you just because they are high traffic.

One word of warning - it can be very intoxicating when you strike gold. Before you start clicking your heels like some old-time prospector or Jed Clampett when he finds there's oil on his farm, just remember that trying to draw traffic to your site for keywords/phrases that you are not relevant for is **not a good idea**.

You'll dilute your position on the phrases you are relevant for at best, pick up a penalty for creating spam content at worst.

Some jobs are like trying to force feed a hedgehog custard. Difficult, messy, pointless, and painful for all concerned.

Why can't I make a list of keywords and then build pages based on that?

You can, sure, but why would you? Is that helping the customer? Probably not.

Sounds like you're doing it because you're trying to please the search engines... breaking one of our fundamental rules in the process. **If you're doing something just to please the search engines... it's probably spam.**

Writing page content (finally!)

Here's what Google has to say about writing good web pages, direct from its own help article on SEO:

"Creating compelling and useful content will likely influence your website more than any of the other factors discussed here. Users know good content when they see it and will likely want to direct other users to it. This could be through blog posts, social media services, email, forums, or other means.

Organic or word-of-mouth buzz is what helps build your site's reputation with both users and Google, and it rarely comes without quality content."

So, there you have it. Write compelling and useful content. It's as simple as that!

Being useful and compelling

"Thomas, you are a really useful engine"
- Sir Topham Hatt, The Fat Controller

If you've followed the steps outlined above, you're already on your way to being *useful* as you've focussed your pages on giving your customers what they want and need.

Hopefully, your content is also **unique**, which we know is important, and up-to-date.

How to spot an unhelpful or boring page

Whilst getting a measure of whether a page is truly "useful" or not may seem a bit nebulous, it is relatively easy to spot a page which is *less useful* than its fellows.

The two key metrics to look at here are **Exit Rate** and **Bounce Rate**.

Pages with high Bounce Rate have customers arriving (landing) on the page and immediately exiting. Pages with high Exit Rate have customers arriving as part of their journey through your site (e.g. they came from another part of your site) and then leaving.

Seeing high numbers in both instances is bad, unless the page is logically the last one in a customer journey (the end of checkout or your 'Contact Us' form are likely to be high-exit rate pages).

By comparison, long viewing times are generally seen as a good metric (assuming that there is a large amount of content on the page). We all have super-short attention spans these days, so keeping someone interested in your page is a small victory in itself.

Customers, turtles, and gate posts

There's an urban legend about a turtle balanced on top of a gatepost that, depending on what website you like to find your urban legend entomology (what, only have one?) probably originates in either Texas or Queensland.

It goes something like this...

"That man's a post turtle."

"What's a post turtle?"

"You know, when you're driving down the road and you see a turtle on top of a gatepost. He doesn't know how he got there, he doesn't know what to do next, and you know he didn't end up there all by himself."

Mostly this is used to insult politicians, but I think it applies pretty well to the average website visitor as well. They land on your site, they don't know where they are or what to do next, and you're the person in charge of sorting that out.

Software developers love the myth of the "stupid user" and will, if you let them, complain at great length about how people don't know how to use computers, shouldn't be allowed to have computers, shouldn't even be allowed near computers, and should probably be replaced with computers in the near future for the good of everyone else.

Here's the reality:

There is no such thing as a stupid user, only bad interface design.

Lots of developers seem to think that it's OK to abandon users who are "too stupid" to use their website/software/app. It's a bizarre behaviour that makes no sense if you transpose it to the real world.

When did you last need to update your smartphone software, or install Flash, or switch to a more up-to-date browser to buy meat at the butcher's shop?

When it comes to web pages my definition of "compelling" for the user is driven by the **Five Second Rule**. (No, not the one about dropping food on the floor).

"The Five Second Rule"

In "The Five Second Rule" Mel Robbins says:

The 5 Second Rule is simple. If you have an instinct to act on a goal, you must physically move within 5 seconds or your brain will kill it.

Assuming this is true (and a *lot* of people following Mel say it is) you've got five seconds per webpage to get the customer to physically move their mouse (or their finger) to click on your call to action, scroll the page to read more content, or have some other form of engagement with your page. Five seconds, **that's it**.

Do those big banner images at the top of web pages that force you to scroll down to see the article make a little more sense now? That's a physical engagement, delivered in under five seconds.

Passing the Five Second Rule Test

To pass the Five Second Rule test, your customer must be able to answer three questions within five seconds of looking at a webpage:

1. What is this page about?
2. Do I think this page contains the answer to my problem?
3. What do I do next?

Or, to look at it another way:

1. What is this page about?
2. Is this page **useful** to me?
3. What action am I **compelled** to take next?

Final tips on content creation

Cheaters never prosper. Never copy content from other websites or use generic content

Duplicate content is anathema to search engines. It's tough enough keeping the content on your site unique *without* stealing content from other people.

Imitation may be the highest form of flattery, but it's not going to get you to the top of a search results page.

Rank best by being best. Look at top ranking content for your keyword and write something more useful

Just because somebody already wrote about a topic and has position #1 on Google, doesn't mean you can't write about it as well.

Take a good look at the pages that rank top for your keywords, read what they have to say, and then write something **more useful and more compelling**.

Video works. Create videos to improve engagement, sharing and pull in traffic from video sharing sites

We've talked a lot about the sort of content you need to write, but video is actually one of the most compelling types of content you can include in your website.

It's OK for your video to be a little "lo-fi" if that fits your tone of voice - take a look at the quality of the average YouTube video... Citizen Kane they are *not*.

Do remember to add subtitles to your videos; a huge amount of video is consumed by users who have their sound *off*.

YouTube will add subtitles to your video automatically, but remember to edit them - the speech recognition is far from perfect.

"85 percent of Facebook video is watched without sound. Facebook might be hosting upwards of 8 billion views per day on its platform, but a wide majority of that viewership is happening in silence. As much as 85 percent of video views happen with the sound off, according to multiple publishers."
- https://digiday.com/media/silent-world-facebook-video/

People still love infographics and are more likely to share these than text

Whilst we're on the topic of visual content, people **still** love infographics. In fact, any content accompanied by a picture is far more likely to generate engagement and be shared, particularly on social media.

Write for humans, not for bots

So far, we've talked a lot about what search engines want.

In fact, we've talked about it **too much**.

Did you ever wonder what would happen if you forgot about search engines altogether and just built the very best website you could? The simplest navigation, the quickest load time, the best content...

Well, if the search engines are to believed - *that's* the site that will be at number one in the search engine ranking.

Remember... **SEO is changing**. Search engines are getting cleverer, faster, and better at presenting the right result. So, there's a simple answer to every SEO question - **be the best result**.

If your digital strategy is to constantly ask "What does Google want?" then you will always be one step behind. Instead, try to answer the question that Google are trying to answer - **what does my customer want?**

The SEO curse of over-optimisation that new SEO people fall for when they are doing SEO to improve their SEO on their SEO website

When people first start working on their SEO, they come across the concept of **keywords**. Then, they start to understand relevance and realise that they haven't been using their keywords and phrases on their website.

And then, sometimes, people go **bananas**.

That person who didn't use their keywords enough:

"This is our best product. When people ask us to make a recommendation, this product is always the one we recommend."

Transforms overnight into someone who uses their keywords so much it feels like they are spraying their content at you from some sort of colossal machine gun loaded with an endless supply of their magic word:

"This **106 key UK layout keyboard** is our best **106 key UK layout keyboard**. When people ask us to recommend a **106 key UK layout keyboard**, this is the **`106 key UK layout keyboard`** that we recommend."

Remember that you are **not** writing content to be read by a machine, you're writing it for a human being.

If in doubt - read it out. Content that sounds strange to you when you read it aloud will not rank well.

Design tips from a non-designer

Clear calls to action

Remember the Post Turtle? Well, the most important part of the five-second rule test is Part 3 - **what action do I take next?**

The thing you want the customer to do on your webpage is called the "call to action". It may look like there's more than one, what with links in the header and footer, menu navigation, search boxes etc. but there should be one, just one, that stands out above all the others.

Your call to action should be like The Highlander... There can be only one!

Amazon does this really well. Take a look at a typical product page on Amazon and there is only **one type of button** that is ever gold... the "Add to Cart" button. Every other option is grey because although Amazon wants you to do them, they want you to add to basket **most of all**.

There's one other thing, not a button, that's gold on that page - and it's the basket.

You know - **the place you go to give them your money.**

Make sure every page has one clear and definitive call to action, even if there are lots of other options for the customer as well.

Avoid too many adverts and banners

On the topic of making your call to action clear, it's advisable not to clutter your web page with adverts, banners and other distracting elements.

If your main call to action is revenue generating - e.g. you will directly benefit from the user taking that call to action - then you should minimise these items to zero.

If your website generates revenue through advertising however, this balance is more difficult to get right. Google created the "Above the Fold" update to penalise websites that were focussing on delivering ads to the reader over delivering content back in 2012, but many websites are still force-feeding adverts to their visitors.

"We've heard complaints from users that if they click on a result and it's difficult to find the actual content, they aren't happy with the experience. Rather than scrolling down the page past a slew of ads, users want to see content right away.

So sites that don't have much content "above-the-fold" can be affected by this change. If you click on a website and the part of the website you see first either doesn't have a lot of visible content above-the-fold, or dedicates a large fraction of the site's initial screen real estate to ads, that's not a very good user experience"

https://search.googleblog.com/2012/01/ page-layout-algorithm-improvement.html

As always, putting the customer's experience first is key. Remember what they came to your website **for** - I'm willing to bet it **wasn't** to see adverts.

Avoid pop-ups and pop-overs. Forever

On the same topic, website pop-ups, pop-overs and "interstitials" are to be avoided at all costs. If you're not sure what these are, you'll recognise one the next time you see one - they are the annoying messages that appear over the content that you went to the website to see asking to sign up to a mailing list, or register, or do something else.

Most customers hate these. Google hates them enough that it updated its algorithm to specifically penalise websites that committed any of the following crimes:

- Showing a popup that covers the main content, either immediately after the user navigates to a page from the search results, or while they are looking through the page.

- Displaying a standalone interstitial that the user has to dismiss before accessing the main content.

- Using a layout where the above-the-fold portion of the page appears similar to a standalone interstitial, but the original content has been inlined underneath the fold.

Interstitials are especially horrible on mobile devices as many of them don't cope well with being resized and reoriented to fit on a mobile screen. Close buttons vanish off the edge of the screen, content fails to load, and everything slows... down.

The result is something the customer doesn't want, sitting on top of the thing they do want, but with no easy to way get rid of it.

Despite how bad a reputation this technique has, people still use it. If I had to take a guess as to *why*, I'd say it is because they **do** work... at least on some people. The mistake people make is to measure the number of people who, for example, sign up to a mailing list without comparing this to the number of users who exit the website completely.

Make sure your address and phone number are on every page of your website. This helps SEO **and** helps your visitors

This may seem obvious. It **should** seem obvious... and yet I see people get this wrong time and time again.

Talking to customers is **good** - so make it easy for them.

The purpose of your website is not to reduce the number of customers contacts that you receive.

Make sure your phone number, address, and link to a contact page are prominent on every page of your website.

Remember to optimise your homepage. Too many homepages are graphics heavy, text light, and hurt SEO

When it comes to homepages, there is a trend at the moment to make these graphics heavy and text light.

It's a bad move, because it reduces your ability to define your product and service on the most frequently visited page of your website.

Would you fill your shop window with posters but no words?

It might work for a fancy boutique, but I prefer to leave an "air of mystery" as the province of ladies with alliterative names who arrive to engage the services of a private eye in the middle of a rainy night.

Your homepage should always be optimised.

Making connections

There's a reason we call them **web** pages - they are designed, fundamentally, to be connected together, like points on a spider's web.

Links from other sites to your sites are referred to as **backlinks**, and we'll talk about those in detail in the next section of the book. Just as important, however, are the ways in which we link pages together within our site.

These links are the ways in which your customer will travel from one page of your site to another, and also the way in which the search engine **spider** will travel.

The way in which you connect one page to another therefore not only affects your SEO but also affects what percentage of customers coming to your website will find what they want and **convert**.

Double. Whammy.

Connections Rules 1: Every page of your site must be linked to another. Search engines won't index pages users can't click to

Search engines are only interested in pages that users can get to.

If you can't navigate to a page simply by clicking links from your homepage, that page is not accessible to your customer or to a search engine.

*Think about it - why would you want to create a page that a **human** couldn't find? Oh... maybe for the **search engine** to find? Great plan but... please go back and read Rule 4.*

Performing this test of your website is about more than just making sure you don't have any hidden pages though. It's about walking a mile (or at least a few clicks) in your customer's shoes and experiencing your website as they will when they visit.

- Keep pages within three clicks of the homepage to maximise your opportunities for conversion.
- Remember that each page has a job to do - identify it and make sure the page content and layout support that role.

And, most importantly, remember that customers don't know where they are going. They may be exploring your site for the first time - so give them multiple opportunities to find what they need by providing multiple routes to content and the opportunity to go backwards as well as forwards on their journey.

Use breadcrumbs, categories, filters, and tags

Search engines like sites that link internally in a variety of ways - creating multiple routes for users to find information and building additional context around the content.

The most common ways to link content together on a website are breadcrumbs, categories, filters, and tags.

Breadcrumbs

Appearing at the top of the page, breadcrumbs show a trail back "up" the website hierarchy to the parent page(s) of the current page.

Your CMS should build this for you - don't even dream of doing this by hand.

Categories

Categories are pages that group together other pages.

The simplest example is a product category page. This might be a type of product ("Vacuum Cleaners") or a brand ("Hoover" or "Dyson").

Category pages are *landing pages* so, as well as links to the other pages in this category, they should have well-optimised content of their own.

Filters

Filters reduce the number of items on a category page.

For example, when looking at vacuum cleaners, you might only be interested in products costing under £200. This is a filter - it's not a page in its own right (this will just create a mess of duplication).

Tags

In the hinterland between categories and filters, are tags. These are often called "hashtags" today - as we use them to group together information on social media by prefixing keywords with a #.

If you use a (hash)tag often, consider making it a category. If you use it infrequently, it's still good to give your user (and search engines) a way of linking together related items even if you aren't going to create a landing page for it.

Avoid excessive links and options

You can lose a customer by offering them too much choice. "Analysis Paralysis" can cost you a sale.

Don't confuse the customer - sell more jam by making fewer flavours.

Human beings love being given choices in threes. "Yes, No, or Maybe" is more palatable than simply "Yes or No" (and, when you think about it, only ⅓ of the options in "Yes, No, Maybe" means no sale - you can still try to convert the "Maybe").

Too many choices however, and our brains can't cope.

Keep it simple and offer the customer clear calls to action.

If the customer gets lost, you've lost the customer.

Literally the final content on content: blogs

Just in case you are still not convinced about the importance of content, let's briefly revisit the equation the calculates website success:

Visits X conversion % X conversion value = return on investment

Of all the strategies for increasing the number of visitors to your website, the creation of new, useful, content is the most powerful and most "evergreen". No matter what new rules and guidelines search engines might introduce in the future, I can't see any logical reason that they would ever, *ever* turn against people creating new and useful content - it is literally the thing that the web is made from.

Content = Rankings. Rankings = Visitors.

So... If you're not blogging... start.

Blogging works. Or, to be more accurate, regularly creating and sharing useful and unique content on your website works.

Blogging is also hard work. I once had a job of writing blog posts about candles. I can tell you now, **not much is changing in the world of candles.** They are pretty much the same as they were last year, the year before that, and three hundred years before that. But, we had to find things to write about and so we found anything and everything we could that could get a "candle" spin on it and we blogged about it.

The hard work paid off. Our rankings improved and our organic traffic improved.

The point is that I'm not giving you advice flippantly or only from the perspective of someone who writes blogs about the fast moving, ever changing technology industry. I'm giving you this advice because it works, because anyone can do it, and because if you're an expert in the field you are working in then you probably do have useful and unique information (or at least a unique perspective) that you can bring to your blog.

Remember...

1. Useful

2. Unique
3. Timely
4. Expert
5. Authoritative
6. Trustworthy

The news

The easiest way to turn up new blog ideas is to find recent news articles related to your keywords and then riff off those. **Don't** just regurgitate the same news article - that might be *timely*, but it's not *useful* or *unique*.

However, if you can add something *useful* and *unique* to the story, you might just strike blogging gold.

During a recent security breach at Facebook, news sites trampled over each other to get the news out. All the usual suspects were there. Where smaller blogs ranked well, even going so far as to appear in Google News (the holy grail of blogging), was in offering advice and guidance to people who may have been affected.

The articles were useful, unique, timely, they used expert knowledge, they were authoritative, and trustworthy. **That's the blogging double trifecta.**

And if you're wondering about those last two factors, there were mostly achieved by being on sites already covering tech, social media, etc. - there's not much point blogging about a Facebook security problem on your blog about baking!

How to eat your own dog food.

The phrase "Eat your own dog food" is believed to have originated inside Microsoft sometime in the 1980s. The concept is that if **you** aren't using your own product, why you expect anyone else to?

"Dogfooding" (as it has become known) can be applied to blogging as well. *Take* your product or service somewhere new, somewhere different, and see how it fairs. Try to do something with your product or service that nobody else has ever done, see what happens, and then *share it*.

You're going to get an interesting story, one way or another.

(And even if you fail, what's to stop you tuning up your product or service and trying again?)

The Prism Trick

Sometimes there is no news, however (see "Nothing ever changes with candles!") and it's here that the Prism Trick can help you generate multiple articles from one small idea...

If you're struggling for a blog idea, try applying the "Prism Trick". I can't remember where I learnt this one, but it's really very useful.

The Prism Trick simply means looking at something we've already seen, but from a different angle or through a different "lens".

If yesterday you blogged about "The 10 Best Scented Candles for your Bathroom", today write about "The 10 Scented Candles to Avoid Using In your Bathroom". Tomorrow, "Unusual Bathroom Fragrances - Candles that shouldn't work..but do!"

This is essentially all the same job in terms of research and brainstorming, but you're going to get three articles out of the one piece of effort.

Like splitting light up through a prism, one thing becomes a multi-faceted many.

Once you have a structure in place, you can also generate new on-topic articles by changing one variable. So, move from the bathroom to the kitchen and you've got three new blog ideas instantly.

Don't be the same - be better, be helpful

You can also look at blogs other people have written. Just because somebody else already wrote an article on a topic doesn't mean you can't write a counterpoint...or **just write something better**.

Another variation of this is to look for questions that people have asked on forums, social media, and Q&A sites that you can answer. There's value in providing the answer right there on the forum, there's even more value to be had in answering the question and writing a longer, more detailed answer on your blog.

Quora, Stack Exchange, and Reddit are all great places to look for questions people are asking. You can even check social media - Twitter's advanced search, for example, lets you look for people asking questions, although your mileage may vary when wading through the tweets of the world.

*The thing to remember is that every question asked on a Q&A site or forum was a Google search **before** it was a question. Nobody posts a question for which they could find the answer. Answering questions is a great way to build up quality blog content that people are actively looking for.*

Of course, you can always share your blog posts on the same forums, sites, and social media networks you are checking for questions. Just sharing and posting, however... that's the internet equivalent of shouting over everyone at a dinner party.

*The Internet should not be a "broadcast" medium - even when sharing your own content you should look to **engage** with the audience: ask questions, ask for feedback, and say thank you for everything you receive.*

Which neatly brings us on to the last part of our ABC (or ACB)... **backlinks.**

B is for Backlinks

Backlinks are incoming links to a webpage from another webpage.

They are, fundamentally, what turns pages into **web**-pages: they are the links, the lines, the plumbing that joins sites together. Without links, there would be no web.

When you see them in that context, it's not surprising that these are pretty important for SEO, right? Scratch that - they are massively important. Massively.

In the past, backlinks were **the** major metric for the ranking of a webpage. A page with a lot of backlinks tended to rank higher on all major search engines, including Google. This is still true, although Google and other search engines have been refining their approach to backlinks - quality has now overtaken quantity and it's no longer simply a matter of getting as many links as you can.

The importance of backlinks cannot be overestimated. Link building is hard, but vital to the success of your website.

*"The only thing worse than being talked about is **not** being talked about"* - Oscar Wilde

The other benefit of backlinks

Before the internet and the World Wide Web, we had backlinks - we just called them "word of mouth" and many people will still tell you that this is the most powerful kind of marketing there is.

Getting a backlink isn't *just* about getting SEO benefits from that link; it's also about getting traffic *through* that link. If you can get a link to your website in front of more people, some of them are going to click that link.

*More links = more traffic, even **without** taking into account SEO.*

OK, so how many of these backlinks do I need?

Sorry, there is no "magic number" of backlinks.

The more backlinks you have the better **as long as** those backlinks are coming in from sites that make sense in context and are relevant to your site.

What the hell does that mean? Let's try an example.

Eggs, milk, cheese, and a locksmith

You have a website where you sell eggs, milk, and cheese. Links from other sites about food and drink would make sense, right? A link from a locksmith's website, by comparison, makes no sense at all. It's pretty unlikely that that link was created *organically*, e.g. without any kind of interference or unnecessary influence, and so we'd call that one out as a backlink that isn't relevant and is therefore worthless.

There's a chance, of course, that the locksmith website *did* have a genuine reason to link to the eggs, milk, and cheese site and this is where *context* comes into play. If the locksmith's website contained a post about putting locks on a new warehouse for the eggs, milk, and cheese site then *that* would have *context*, even if the site itself wasn't that relevant. I'd expect this link to have low value, but it may pass some small value on to the site that it is linking to.

If you ever had to make a mindmap in school, that's what the world wide web is *supposed* to look like - one topic linked to another related topic, with subtle changes from page to page eventually linking disparate items.

You may be only six degrees of separation from Kevin Bacon, but your website probably isn't. Sorry, Kevin.

Quality trumps quantity with backlinks - although personally, I don't think you should be making a choice between one and the other. What's wrong with having a large number of high-quality links?

Answer: **Nothing**. It's just a pretty hard thing to achieve.

The Three Golden Rules of Backlinking

To spot a "good" backlink, apply this simple three point test:

1. The easier a backlink is to get, the less value it probably has.

2. Never, **ever** buy backlinks.

3. Never, **ever** get involved in link swaps, link shares, link rings, link directories, or putting your links in a bowl at a party and taking somebody else's link out at the end of the night.

Places you don't want links from:

1. Sites that are irrelevant to your site.

Shockingly, backlinks from irrelevant sources are... irrelevant. Focus on building links in your niche and vertical market.

2. Untrustworthy sites.

Backlinks from untrustworthy sites are... untrustworthy. If you wouldn't click a link on *that site nobody* else will either. Even search engines know to avoid a "sketchy neighbourhood".

Diversify your backlinks. Different types of links from different types of sites builds more value.

3. Other sites that you also own.

Creating another site and then using that site to link to your own site is frowned upon by Google. People used to employ tricks like creating a "blog.domainx.com" site to link to "www.domainx.com" or even creating whole other websites to generate links to their main site.

All of these are bad ideas and contravene one of our golden rules: never do anything *just* to trick a search engine.

How to get backlinks

"So, I'm not allowed to buy them, swap them, or sign up to a service that provides them… how the hell am I supposed to get backlinks then?"

The "company line" answer from Google is to create a great website full of great content and let links organically come to you. There's a reason that we covered content *before* backlinks, you see.

However, whilst it is entirely possible for this strategy to work, there is no guarantee that backlinks are magically going to arrive. There is no backlinks fairy, *as far as I know…*

If you want backlinks, you're going to have to do some work to generate them.

Talk to existing contacts for backlinks

Yes, it's OK to ask someone for a link.

The first, and easiest, way to get backlinks is to talk to people you know and see if they are happy to post an article on their website that includes a link to you. You can even provide the article; a technique called "Guest Blogging" which we will cover in a bit more detail below.

This may seem a bit "needy", but you've got to start somewhere and you are missing a trick if you don't reach out to business contacts, friends, and connections who would be willing to link to your site **without** a link back in return.

Prolific crowdfunder Amanda Palmer released a fascinating TED Talk and book about "The Art of Asking", which is where I've pillaged this quote from:

"Those who can ask without shame are viewing themselves in collaboration with - rather than competition with - the world"
- Amanda Palmer

In short, "**You don't ask, you don't get**".

Remember, search engines are looking for links from *relevant sites* that are *in context*, so it's only worth approaching contacts who are working in your own industry.

Talk to people you don't know

Remember the various techniques that we talked about for coming up with ideas for your blog? Wouldn't it be great if someone just contacted you, out of the blue, with an interesting piece of news that was relevant to your site that you could blog about?

Sending your content to relevant sites to highlight what you're doing because it might be relevant to them is 100% OK when it comes to backlink building.

This technique is hardly rocket science however, so don't expect to be the one and only email that a large website in your niche/sector receives that day. Just as you need to make your contact engaging, useful, and timely for visitors, you need to do the same for the people you are going to be sending your content to in the hope that they will read it, like it, and link to it.

"If you want to catch more fish, use more hooks"
- George Allen Snr

Be sure to spread your wings - don't rely on just one or two sites. Make it your business to know the websites that are prominent in your sector and get your content to them, but don't overlook smaller or quieter sites and don't give up if the larger sites don't carry your content straight away. Building backlinks is like any other kind of networking - you may need to build up your profile over a series of interactions before you gain any traction.

The "Broken Link" Trick

There's a trick that's been doing the rounds for a while in linking building circles. I'm not a huge fan of it, but it would be wrong to leave it out.

The trick relies on finding websites that have out of date or broken links and then writing to the owner of that site to point out the problem and offer your site as a replacement.

You can download extensions for Google Chrome and other web browsers that will check a webpage for broken links - simply point the tool at a page relevant to yours and check to see if there are any broken links.

Check my Links Tool for Google Chrome: https://chrome.google.com/webstore/detail/check-my-links/ojkcdipcgfaekbeaelaapakgnjflfglf?hl=en-GB

This technique relies on the person receiving your message being grateful that you've pointed out the problem with their website and accepting your link as a replacement. The content of the contact email is all important in this context.

Personally, I have not used this technique in bulk, but when researching additional techniques for this section of the book I kept coming across this method time and again, so it certainly seems to be popular with some SEO consultants.

Press releases

A more traditional approach to getting your content out there is to use press releases.

"A press release is a short, compelling news story written by a public relations professional and sent to targeted members of the media. The goal of a press release is to pique the interest of a journalist or publication."

Like a message about any other piece of content, press releases can be sent directly to websites, blogs, etc. There are also specific services available for the "syndication" of press releases that will put your press release in front of a wide array of journalists and publications from a single upload.

There are free and paid versions of these services; if you're going to look at using these then the paid option is the best way to go. Like any marketing channel however, you should track how well your content does when you pay for syndication - if you can't see a return on your investment, try a different strategy and/or change up your content.

Steal your competitors' backlinks. Look at where their best links come from and chase a link from there

Now, this one sounds a bit more nefarious than it is.

Let's say you're currently cooling your heels down at number 11 for a particular search term. (That means you're on the second page, the "wrong side of the tracks" of search engine results). Meanwhile, you've got a competitor who is in position 1, right up there on the first page, where all the people are and clicks are.

As we've already established, there will be lots of different factors contributing to them being at #1 and you at #11, and backlinks **will** be one of them.

It's relatively easy to find out which sites are linking to others. Google used to let you do this direct from the search bar, but that's become a bit less reliable of late so you'll want to use a third party tool like Moz's Link Explorer:

https://moz.com/link-explorer/

Simply by entering a competitor URL into Link Explorer, you can get a list of the sites that are linking to them. Guess what… they might want to link to you as well.

Remember, however, that just because your competitor has a link from a particular site *doesn't mean* that that link is a good link. Don't assume that your competitor knows what they are doing.

Understanding how your competitors have approached link building can be a hugely informative process though and it's something you should be looking at on a regular basis.

Try finding sites you don't know about!

Up until now, we've built every link from using something we already know as a "jumping off point". It may sound obvious, but I am going to point something out here that you've hopefully already thought of.

You can Google sites in your sector and niche, just like a customer does. The best sites to get links from are going to be near the top of the list, because that's where Google puts them.

Try combining your search keywords with terms like "news", "chat", "questions", "network", "help", and "blog" to find the people talking about your keywords.

Other things that look like backlinks but aren't

There are a couple of other very important ways of getting links to your content that look a lot *like* backlinks, but aren't - **advertising** and **social media**.

I'll talk about those in a little while...

Link building hacks

Here are some final thoughts and tips on link building before we talking about ads and social media...

Don't just build backlinks to your homepage. Backlink to any page you want to rank and see benefits.

You don't only have to chase links to your homepage/domain. Getting internal links can be just as good, especially if they deliver traffic directly to a relevant page.

If you have a strong internal linking setup (see "Breadcrumbs, Categories, and Tags" above) then the internal pages that receive "Link Juice" from other sites will pass some of that juice onto the pages it is linked to.

Don't stuff backlinks with keywords. Keyword backlinks are high value, but too many is unnatural.

If you are in a situation where the person/site linking to you is asking you what you would like the link text to be, I'd be inclined to say that you are on shaky ground anyway as that doesn't sound a lot like an "organic" link.

If you do find yourself in this place, however, don't be tempted to cram that backlink text with keywords. It's a clear sign of a spammy link.

The most organic looking link will be to your site's name or brand name.

*If you were going to recommend your friend Mike the Plumber to somebody, you would say "Try calling Mike" or "Try calling Mike's Pipes" not "**Try calling Best and Cheapest Plumber in Cardiff Swansea Cardiff**".*

Take link building offline. A phone call goes much further than an email or a tweet when link building

Most people running websites understand the value of a backlink. If you're not giving them something (like some great content for their site) then you're asking them for something valuable. There's nothing wrong with that **at all**, but you may find you are more successful if you reach out to them in real life (or "IRL" as the kids say).

Don't use comments to link build but do use comments to network. Take part in your community

One of the oldest and most maligned of link building "hacks" is to post comments on other peoples' websites that include your website address. It's a process that has been heavily automated by evil SEO types and is the bane of many a blog and website. If you allow users to comment on your website, you've probably found spam comments posted there.

I don't have a special method to make this work for you. **Just don't do it.**

You should, however, make a conscious effort to take part and contribute to communities and groups online that contain other people working in your industry/niche/vertical. There's a reason that it's called the inter**net**. It's a network, and you can use it to network.

Just like your own content, your comments should be as useful, unique, and timely as possible. Build up a positive reputation and support others and you will find organic links appear more readily to your own content.

Sites may link to sites but those links are built by people - and people link to other people.

Most online directories are worthless, but seek out those relevant to your industry, niche, and location

The importance of links created something of a "gold rush" back in the old days of the Internet from which I come...

It was in a time before social media, when people ate food without taking a picture of it, a "Facebook" was something that serial killers probably had in their basement, and people were building internet directories by the bucket-load...

The most venerable of these sites were places like Yahoo!, DMoz, and Lycos. These sites provided long lists of categorised links to other sites, like an Internet Yellow Pages. There was even a time when you could buy a hardcopy directory of the web, printed and bound in an actual book. Dark times indeed.

Still, directory bred directory bred directory and the dustier corners of the web are still occupied by these things. Most of them are worthless - they have low SEO value themselves, low traffic, and won't amount to much of anything if you do get a link from them.

The only directories now worth looking at in terms of backlinking are the well organised, large directories (like the *actual* Yellow Pages, which in the UK now calls itself "Yell") or very niche directories maintained enthusiastically by, well, enthusiasts.

Most of the enthusiasts have moved to social media now, leaving the big directories as the only game in town. If you're in the right kind of industry then these are worth looking at but if you're not doing the sort of thing people would normally look in the Yellow Page for - there's no good reason to be in the Yellow Pages.

Nobody advertises pork chops in a vegan cookery magazine.

Outbound links

Google likes sites that take part in the "egalitarian web", so don't fear linking to other useful sites and don't listen to scare-mongers who will tell you that you're "leaking link juice".

While we are on the topic, "link juice" has to be one of the worst metaphors in the history of the web. I'd rather it were "Tiger Tokens" or anything else that didn't sound like it would ruin your best shirt if you got it on you.

Don't be afraid to link out to other sites that complement yours or would be relevant to your readers/visitors. Nobody in their right mind is going to link to a direct competitor, but that doesn't mean that you can't provide some *useful and informative* links to other sites.

Wait a minute... What about "cost per click" ads?

Aren't adverts the ultimate paid for link? You wouldn't be 100% wrong there...

Remember what we learnt in Chapter 1 - the only **guaranteed** way to have the #1 result on the front page of Google is to **pay Google**. Same goes for Bing, Yahoo!, DuckDuckGo, and any other search engine you care to mention.

Google, through its search engine at least, only sells two things:

1. To consumers, it sells answers to questions.

2. To businesses, it sells the opportunity to be the answer to a question.

Paying for adverts will increase your traffic. End of story.

Paying for adverts does not, contrary to many a good conspiracy theory, improve your SEO.

Good SEO **does** reduce the cost of your adverts however, thanks to a little something called The Quality Score.

"Quality score is an estimate of the quality of your ads, keywords and landing pages. Higher quality ads can lead to lower prices and better ad positions." - https://support.google.com/google-ads/answer/140351?hl=en-GB

That's as direct from the virtual horse's mouth as it gets and the key thing to spot there is that it's not just how good your advert is, but how good your **landing page** is.

In short, the more relevant your page is to the keyword you are advertising for, the better your quality score will be.

If you want to know definitively, on a scale of 0-10, how relevant Google thinks your page is to a particular keyword then Quality Score is about as close as you are going to get.

Keep in mind that Quality Score is also affected by how good your advert is - you're not getting completely behind the wizard's curtain here. You can at least *see* the curtain though, and that's a start.

Is that it? You're not going to tell me any more about CPC?

Afraid so - this is a book about SEO and the one thing I **promised** you in Chapter 1 was that everything I suggest in this book would be completely free for you to do. You've got to invest some work, some blood-sweat-and-tears time, but not one penny (or cent) down.

Tip: You can even use most of Google Ads for free - sign up but don't put any money down. You'll be amazed at how much data you can still access.

One more thing - you can actually get a backlink from Google...

If you search for a business by name, Google will try to "surface" (posh word "show") a "Google My Business" entry in the sidebar of the search results.

Whilst this isn't a backlink in the normal sense of the word, it's a really important thing to make sure you're in control of and have optimised - if you are a "real world" business then your Google My Business entry is going to be seen by anyone who searches for your business **before** they see your website.

Reviews are particularly important here. You could have a website full of great customer testimonials but if your Google My Business rating is poor then you can expect that to have a big impact on the number of click-throughs you will see from search.

Not taking control of your Google My Business listing is like letting some random person put the signs on the outside of your building, design and distribute business cards and fliers you've never seen, and then dress your shop window.

It's not Google's job to give you the *best* listing they can - it's their job to give the most *accurate* listing they can with the data they have.

Social media and backlinks

It's one of the **big questions** that gets the SEO conspiracy theorists running for their post-it notes and balls of string... do search engines index social media?

If the social network in question is Twitter, the answer is a definitive "yes". Back in 2015 Google and Twitter inked a deal that gave Google access to Twitter's data and Google began embedding Tweets into the search engine results page when dealing with "trending" topics.

If you want to see this in action, just search Google for "What is trending right now?" and you'll see Twitter results at the top of the search engine page.

Today's "trending topic" is tomorrow's fish and chip wrapper though (or something like that), so it's doubtful that appearing in this part of the SERP does anything long term for your SEO.

What it will do, if you strike gold and find your tweet on the front page of Google is generate traffic. We talk *so much* in the SEO world about link building to improve SEO we sometimes forget that people **can actually click your backlinks**. They're not just for search engines and, for me, that sums up what social media is all about.

Social media is a firework

There's an adage that circulates on the web...

"The internet is forever"

And, unless you can convince everyone everywhere to delete your data, that's true.

Print and be damned? Forget it. Tweet and be damned for all eternity...

But, although all of that data is there in the vast and unlimited memory of the internet, the reality is that your social media posts have a shorter half-life than an unstable radioactive isotope.

A typical tweet, without retweets, will stop being seen after 18 minutes. With 10 retweets, you might last nearly 24[1].

That's why I say that social media is like a firework - you need to get a big bang for people to remember it past the *next* thing they see.

So, what's the point?

Background radiation

There's no doubt that brands with good social media followings gain more traffic online and sell more. Whilst your tweet, Instagram picture, or Facebook post may only have a short lifespan in the digital feed that a customer sees, it has a much longer lifespan in their memory.

---

[1] https://mtomconsulting.com/lifespan-social-media-post/

I like to think of this as a kind of "background radiation" - constantly reinforcing your brand's identity with customers make it more likely that they will engage when you present a piece of content that is relevant to them *at a time that it is relevant.*

You can't just send out one tweet and expect the dollars to come rolling in.

I've had my own short stints in the past where I've walked away from social media however and know from my own experience that when you do this, that background radiation fades away. Contacts get harder to make, meetings get harder to land, pitches feel colder.

"Brand Awareness" may sound like a perfectly immeasurable, ephemeral, ethereal piece of marketing guff, a piece of "ghostware" for the snake oil salesman and charlatans to sell you but... **it's real**.

Social media impact can be hard to measure, even with the best tools to attribute sales to social engagement weeks or even months after the "first touch" on social.

I prefer to measure in terms of the amount of serendipity I am experiencing in any one period, and this undoubtedly increases when I am active on social media.

Never pull the plug on your social media.

It's not all about me (or you)

It's very easy to get stuck in a pattern of "broadcasting" on social media, rather than creating conversations and connections.

As a rule of thumb, you should comment on or share five things **from other people** for every one thing of your own that you share.

Some of my most successful pieces of social content have been responses to other people's posts. So, answer questions, offer your opinion, and above all *be helpful.*

The same rules of content apply - make it useful, make it unique, retain your authentic tone of voice. Just don't be "that guy" (or girl) at the party who only talks about themselves all night.

Write once, publish often

It should go without saying at this point that once you've created a great piece of content, you should share it on as many relevant social media channels as possible.

What makes a network relevant? I don't believe in ignoring a particular network because you think it's demographic might not be right for your product, but you should tailor the content to the network that you are sharing it to.

For example:

1. Facebook users tend to like funny, inspirational, or "soft" content.

2. LinkedIn users tend to like more serious content and the opportunity to offer their opinion.

3. Instagram, being picture driven, requires little text but a powerful visual.

There's no reason to think that the Facebook user, Instagram user, and LinkedIn user are not all **the same person** in this example; but they are operating in a different "mode" when they are on each network and the more you can tailor the content to that network the better your chances of creating engagement.

This doesn't necessarily mean *changing* the content, just the way you share it.

For example, for a new product launch:

1. On Facebook post pictures of the team celebrating the launch of the new product - tag those who are on Facebook and show your customers (and competitors) what a great team and business you have.

2. On LinkedIn publish more details on the product and what you think it is going to do for your business, the industry at large, etc. Reach out to influencers (more on that later) and industry experts to try to get their opinion

3. On Instagram post product shots and try to get customers to share pictures of them using the product with you

"Content is fire, social media is gasoline." - Jay Baer

On the topic of sharing, there's also nothing wrong with publishing content more than once.

"What?" I hear you cry (well, I don't but...) "What about duplication. You told us about a hundred times that duplication is bad!"

And, yes, this is true. If you post the exact same content to multiple websites you're going to devalue your content and create duplication issues for yourself.

However...

Most social networks are "walled gardens" - you have to have a login to see some (or any) any of the content and, as we've already established, the lifespan of a "share" is brief.

The people leading the field in "social selling" have a back catalogue of content and they frequently repost older content either with a new "hook" - relating it to current events, a piece of business news, or in response to a question they have been asked - or just as a "you may not have seen this" or "here's one of our most popular videos".

Most social networks algorithms don't appear to have a massive issue with reposted content **if it generates engagement.**

So, don't worry too much if you mistime the posting of your next video. You can try again in a few days at a different time.

The ultimate backlink - the returning customer

Before we leave backlinks behind, I'd like to circle back around and revisit what an organic link really is - **it's a vote of confidence.**

Of all the people on the internet (and there are quite a few of them) the ones you should want a backlink from more than any others are your customers.

It's a well-established fact that it's cheaper to retain an existing customer and get repeat business from them than to acquire a new customer. The ratio you'll see quoted a lot online is that it's **five times more expensive to acquire a new customer than to sell to an existing one.**

So, whilst most of this book has been about using SEO techniques to *increase* your business, find *new* customers, and make *new* sales - **never forget the customers that you have**.

- Create new content **for them**; answer their questions and address their issues.

- Engage **with them** on social media and **share their content.**

- Share more useful content with them via email lists.

- Take their feedback on your website and implement changes that will benefit them.

Bill Gates once said…

"Your most unhappy customers are your greatest source of learning"

and if you ever used Windows Vista or Windows 8, you'll see how Bill Gates got so smart.

The murky world of influencer backlinks

Influencer marketing has been one of the hottest trends in digital marketing of recent years. You've probably come across influencers, you may even have been "influenced" by one, but you maybe didn't realise it...

Influencers are like people, but they exist inside a hyper-stylised twenty-four hour a day live roleplaying game that takes place in the real world.

Instagram is **full** of influencers - people who build up large follower counts and then charge brands to feature their products in a positive light in their social media.

The first thing to understand is that influencer marketing is **not** new. In the 1760s, Josiah Wedgwood and Sons, producers of pottery and chinaware, used royal endorsements as a marketing device to show value in the company and promote others their product.

In the 1930s, brands pursed athletes for endorsements. By the 40s movie stars had begun to replace athletes as the "go to" for endorsements. In the 60s TV stars and entertainers entered the fray... the list goes on.

"People influence people. Nothing influences people more than a recommendation from a trusted friend. A trusted referral influences people more than the best broadcast message. A trusted referral is the Holy Grail of Advertising." - Mark Zuckerberg

In the 1980s, Nike pinned their colours to the rising star of Michael Jordan, and if I recall correctly pretty much every child of the 80s wanted a pair of Nike Air Jordans. They had air **in the sole of the shoe**. It made walking like flying. Kids today just don't understand…

The point is that *today* we've reached a point where you don't need to be an athlete, movie star, TV star, or have air in the soles of your shoes to be a celebrity. Social media has very conveniently quantified our exact level of influence by counting our "friends" and "followers" and a system now exists where **anyone** can be a celebrity.

This has led to the explosion of "influencer marketing" - which is just another way of saying "endorsements".

Bad Influence

So, getting an influencer to recommend your product is good, right?

Short answer - **yes**. Long answer - yes, **if you do it properly**.

Unfortunately, influencer marketing has a very murky side: YouTube stars who have been less than honest with their followers about *why* they are recommending a product (prompting new guidelines and a "product placement disclosure tool" to be implemented back in 2016), influencers whose vast follower counts have turned out to be just an endless stream of fake "bots", and social media superstars who have crashed and burned in epic ways after releasing controversial or offensive content.

It's not just the "little guys" who get this wrong either - Pepsi's phenomenally expensive Kendal Jenner advert which was such a political misstep that it was pulled completely little more than 24 hours after being released in the face of public outcry online. Turns out, there are some ideas that are so bad even a Kardashian can't salvage them.

The internet is fickle.

A good influencer, someone who truly understands your brand and who buys into it can be transformative for your brand. In this respect, the best influencer marketing is like the best backlinks - it occurs organically. Anything manufactured or bought or engineered into being, especially anything that goes against the influencer's own brand, is going to be less effective in the long run.

Bottom line: You should be doing everything you can to get your product in front of the most influential people in your industry, niche, or sector.

Great influencer marketing isn't paying influencers to endorse your brand - it's winning the influencer the way you win a customer; with great content, great products, and great service.

How Do I Know If Any Of This Is Working?

Pretty important question, right?

Good news! There are a huge range of services out there that you can plug into your website to help you understand where your visitors are coming from, what they are doing when they are on your site, and how you can (at least try) to get more of them.

Every run of these tools will promise you the Earth in terms of SEO but remember - they don't have any special insight into your website that you don't have. **Every** analytical platform relies on data being passed to them by your website. They can only work with the data you give them and so, in reality, they aren't telling you anything you don't already know.

What good analytics platforms do do is help you marshal and interpret the data from your website and, hopefully, turn it into actionable insights.

Despite this all being pretty logical, I've seen websites running tens of analytical and tracking platforms simultaneously - utterly ridiculous.

Personally, I like to keep things simple and use a small set of tried and tested tools.

There's no point running more analytical platforms than you have the time and skills required to monitor.

Google Analytics

The king of analytical software and something no website should be without.

Completely free, extremely easy to implement, there is no excuse for not having Google Analytics on your website.

This doesn't mean *understanding* what is in your analytics reports will be easy so, again, my recommendations is to keep it simple.

1. Use Google Analytics to look at the key metrics that define website performance; number of visitors, conversion percentage, conversion value, and total revenue.

2. Drill down into one variable at a time - where the visitor came from (their channel), where they started out (their landing page) and look for patterns

3. Look for under-performing scenarios, such as one landing page that isn't converting as many customers as others, and make a change to try and improve your website

4. Wait...

5. Re-check your analytics to see if your change has made things better... or worse.

Yes, it's **literally** this simple. The trick, or the "art" if you prefer, is to spot the patterns in the first place.

I could write a whole book on spotting patterns in Google Analytics (I probably *will*, one day) but, for now, these are a few common factors you should always be looking into:

1. **Traffic Source:** Where did the visitor come from? Was it a search engine, a link in a tweet, your cost-per-click campaign?

2. **Landing Page:** What page did they start their journey on?

3. **Device Type:** What type of device (desktop, laptop, tablet, mobile, etc.) was the customer using?

Murder on the Analytics Express

If I had £1 for every time someone had said to me "our sales are up/down because of X", where X was one thing and they hadn't bothered to look at any other factors... well, I wouldn't need to be writing SEO books anymore. I'd be on a beach somewhere, writing books about something else entirely.

The point is, it's **easy** to latch onto the first link you find between (let's say) site speed and conversions. "Page load times went up and conversions went down". Seems logical. **Is** logical. But is it the whole story?

What if conversions had been slipping down for *months*, but the site had only slowed down since the last software update? What if traffic had also dropped, or a popular product had gone out of stock or been taken off the market, or you'd stopped spending money on CPC this month?

Much like the conclusion to Murder on the Orient Express (no spoiler apology, if you haven't read it then you've brought this on yourself) - there's often more than one culprit.

Don't get sucked in by your first deduction - be sure that you've looked at the problem from more than one angle.

"Unless you are good at guessing, it is not much use being a detective."
- Agatha Christie

Land then Bounce, Exit or Convert

When looking at your analytics data, remember that there are three possible outcomes to every visit: Bounce, Exit, or Convert.

Bounce: The visitor leaves without going to another any other page - they literally "bounce off" your website.

Exit: The visitor leaves, but this is *not* the first page that they looked at.

Convert: Huzzah! The customer converted. They will now exit, but you got the conversion.

All three are normal states, but obviously we want to

1. Reduce the number of bounces to be as low as possible

2. Have the minimum number of non-converting exits

Attribution Models

Not every visit that ends in a bounce or an exit without a conversion is necessarily a failure. Depending on your particular industry or niche, it may require multiple visits to your website before the customer will convert.

Thinking more broadly, it's a well-established marketing principle that it takes seven "touches" before someone will be ready to interact on a call to action. These touches can be online or offline, such as

- A physical connection, such as meeting at a networking event

- Seeing an ad, either physical or digital

- Seeing your logo, maybe as a sponsor or on a brochure

- Seeing your social media posts in a news stream

- Receiving your e-newsletter or other email marketing piece

- A phone call

- A word-of-mouth mention by a friend or colleague

- Visiting your website

Google offers a special type of report, the "Attribution Model" that allows you to see which online touches have taken place in the run up to a conversion.

If you're unsure, for example, of what contribution your social media activity is having on sales the Attribution Model will be able to show you.

Using this model you can control the timeline over which the interactions have taken place, my preference is for a 90-day window, and whether conversions are allocated to the first interaction, last interaction, or proportionally across multiple interactions.

When you are looking at a "normal" Google report you are already looking at a "Last Interaction" report - if the report tells you the traffic source is (for example) email then *that* is the last interaction. This is why I like to look at **First Interaction** on my conversions - this is the interaction that is doing the hard work of creating interest in a website/brand for the very first time with a customer.

Advice on Time Travel

When conducting comparisons of **any** statistic, it is important to take into account the times that you are comparing.

Many businesses will have seasonal fluctuations in their sales - it's not rational therefore to always compare this month to last month. Most businesses will *want* to look at month to month statistics, but comparing the past month to the same month in the previous year is more logical.

Don't fall into the trap of comparing apples with oranges (or Mays with Decembers).

The Cookie Monster Paradox

I mentioned a little earlier the problem of running *too many* analytics platforms.

Not only is it a waste of time (unless you have an army of people to interpret all that data) but it's also having a negative impact on your website performance. Most analytics tools need to deposit a cookie (a small text file of information) onto your computer to help them remember you from page to page and visit to visit. Google Analytics is no exception.

I've been using a tool called **Ghostery** (https://www.ghostery.com/) which tells me what tracking technologies websites are using and allows me to block them, if I want to, based on these cookies.

The most incredible thing that I've noticed using this utility is how much **faster** the web becomes when I'm not using **my bandwidth** to shovel data to umpteen third party tracking platforms that have been integrated into websites that I visit.

Like me, you're probably already sick of cookie pop-ups asking you to complete complex preference arrangements on websites. Here's my tip - install a cookie blocker like Ghostery and you'll never need to worry about being tracked online again. You'll also save bandwidth and have a faster internet.

"It's impossible to move, to live, to operate at any level without leaving traces, bits, seemingly meaningless fragments of personal information."
- William Gibson

Can't someone else do it?

If your website provider cares about you, they will make sure that you have access to Google Analytics and they will make sure you are getting regular reports.

*If your website provider is one of the snake-blooded sort who are secretly reptiles wearing human skin... then they will send you the reports once a month **and** charge you for the privilege.*

Either way, make sure **you** have the ability to log in and at least explore your analytics. You wouldn't run your business without checking your accounts on a regular basis, would you?

Google Search Console

Google Search Console is like Google Analytics' less popular, nerdier cousin.

Instead of telling you what is happening on *your* website, it tells you what is happening on search - and it is therefore an invaluable resource in terms of finding out how well your site is doing in terms of appearing in search engine results pages (SERP) at Google, how many clicks you are getting and, most importantly of all, **what search terms are putting your website in front of customers.**

At a minimum, make sure you can:

1. Access Google Search Console

2. Get a list of search results, clicks, and search engine position

3. Filter this report to *your country*

That third point is of crucial importance. Google presents a different search index in different countries but, weirdly, aggregates that data in Search Console into a single value. You will (or should!) always rank best on your "home turf" so make sure that you filter the data you are looking at to the country you are based in.

Where to focus in Google Search Console

The vast majority of clicks go to the first few results on the first page of Google's results. After that, the number of clicks drops precipitously. In fact, a lot of people will **try a different search instead of going to page 2.**

The last time I had to go to page 2 of Google's results I felt as if I was walking down the alleyway where Batman's parents got shot. If you want to hide a dead body, hide it on page 2 of Google's search results.

So, if you are looking for "bang for your buck" when it comes to changes to your website, look for search terms or pages that are lurking just off the front page (position 11 and onwards, usually). Getting a page from page 2 to page 1 can have a serious impact on your traffic.

Equally, pages that are lurking low on the first page can become superstars if you can just give them a little boost. Positions 1 to 3 are the holy grail. And, as an added bonus when you get there, you probably knocked one of your competitors out of there as well!

"Schadenfreude is so nutritious."
- Will Self

Google My Business

An increasing number of searches are *local* - a trend that has only been growing since the mobile internet and smartphones came to prominence. Today, more than half of web traffic comes from mobile devices and, therefore, it makes a lot of sense that Google surface a special type of search result, called "Google My Business", if a company or business matches the search in question. We mentioned this before in "Backlinks".

Getting a Google My Business listing is completely free - just head over to https://www.google.com/intl/en_uk/business/

and register. Be ready to verify your business either with a phone call or a piece of old-school paperwork through the mail.

Once you are registered you will be able to control, to a degree, how your business is presented including:

- ☐ Your address
- ☐ Your phone number
- ☐ Your opening hours
- ☐ Pictures of your business (inside and out)
- ☐ and **reviews of your business**

Reviews of your business on Google My Business are incredibly important - they are likely to be one of the first things a new prospective customer will see.

Trustpilot and TripAdvisor may have cornered the market temporarily in online reviews and Google is known to syndicate this data **but**, if you're looking for a "mystic Chris" prediction for the future - expect Google to eventually default to using only its own data for star ratings against websites, once the amount of data reaches a "critical mass" and the data from third parties is no longer required.

Any business that offers a service through someone else's platform that can be replicated by that platform will eventually either be bought by, or put out of business by, that platform.

You like me, you really like me...

It may seem needy but asking your existing customers for a review on Google My Business is an extremely worthwhile exercise. Often, a simple prompt to leave a review is all that it takes.

These are all Google tools - what about the others?

Google holds around **85%** of the search engine market.

Read that again… **85%**.

It's true they are not the only game in town (you'll find a little more on this later!) but you'd be insane if you didn't acknowledge that the vast majority of searches in **you want to appear for** are going to happen on Google's search engine.

Start there.

Tips, Tricks, and Reminders

OR

"Things that wouldn't fit anywhere else in the otherwise orderly and perfect structure of my book"

AND

"Things I want you to think about one more time"

Always do both on-site SEO and off-site SEO and make them complimentary. Don't limit your success

There are two types of SEO - **on-site** and **off-site**.

On-site SEO relates to things that you do... on your site. These might be technical changes, content changes, structural things, etc. These are the things that are the easiest to control and to influence, because you control your site.

Off-site SEO relates to things that are happening on *other people's* websites. This includes link building, social networking, interfacing with third party channels. These things are harder to work on, because you won't have as much control, but they can often be more beneficial.

Think of it this way...

You've built the best shop in the world (on-site SEO) but nobody bothered to put an advert in the paper or tell anyone you were open (off-site SEO). Your shop is not very busy...

It's easy to fall into the trap of only doing one kind of SEO, usually the one that is easiest for you or the one where you get the quickest results with the least effort. But, by doing this, you're limiting the number of opportunities you have to succeed.

My advice is this - **do both on-site and off-site SEO.**

Typically, on-site SEO will pay back quicker - especially on a website that has structural, technical, or content issues. Off-site SEO may take longer to pay back, will pay back *bigger*, generally speaking.

If you're not doing SEO yet… start today. If you are doing SEO, do some today, and every day after that. Any day you lose is a day your competition gains

Did I mention yet that you need to **do SEO**?

I hope so.

You also need to do it today. Start today, literally today, with any improvement you can make to your website, any new piece of content you can add, or any opportunity you can find to get an inbound link, social media share, or comment from a third on or about your site.

Then… do the same tomorrow.

Because **SEO is changing** there will always be something to do and you should aim to do that thing, whatever it is, today (or as soon as possible) because, if you don't, there's a chance your competition will. Even if they don't, it means *your strategy* is going to be a day behind where it could have been.

The web moves **fast.**

A good SEO project isn't a "project" at all. Projects have a beginning, a middle, and an end. SEO can't be that because as soon as you stop, your competition starts to catch up. Stop too long, and they overtake you.

Good SEO is a habit. Great SEO is culture. It all starts with a first day.

Some sharks die if they stop swimming. Be the shark. Swim.

Know your enemy. What the sites are ranking 1st page for your keywords and how did they get there?

I've talked a lot about needing to do better, faster SEO because if you don't your competitors will. There's another important point I need to make about competitors - **make sure you know who they are**.

Now, you may *think* you know who your competitors are, but if you're only worried about the company down the road that does the same thing as you then you're *not* thinking like an SEO.

Your number one, two, and three competitors are the number one, two, and three search results that appear on Google when you search for what it is you do - these websites will take a vast majority of the search traffic when people are looking for your product or service on the internet.

There's nothing wrong with looking at what your competitors do well and then doing the same, but better. I guarantee your strongest competitors are doing this to each other and probably to you as well.

Local SEO and why you do need to worry about that company down the road after all...

Google, and other search engines, are always looking for new ways to improve their search results. One of these improvements has been "local SEO" - ensuring that if you search for something then preference is given to results that are nearby to you if Google thinks that proximity matters.

This means there is actually more than **one** number one slot available. You don't need to be the number result for "24 hour plumber" on all of Google, you just need to be the number one result for "24 hour plumber" for people in your immediate area.

Localisation isn't the only way that Google will personalise search results either - they will use your own search history as well. You're actually more likely to see your own site than a competitor's (assuming you click yourself in search results - and we all do).

Here's the science bit...

The best way to get an unbiased view of how well you are doing in search engine rankings is to use Google's own **Search Console**. Failing this, at least run your searches in Google Chrome's **incognito mode**, which will disable some of the history and tracking features.

No two sites are the same. Don't rely blindly on a strategy just because it worked for someone else

So, it's as simple as looking at what the number one company is doing and doing the same as them? Awesome, put the book down and get down to some hardcore plagiarism... **or not.**

Thankfully for those of us who have worked hard to position sites by creating great content, embracing technical SEO (more on *that* later), and putting in the hours on off-site SEO and link-building, just copying and pasting what we've already done isn't going to get you anywhere.

In fact, it might just land you with a **penalty** and a no-stops trip to search engine hell.

Google has a well-known aversion to duplicate content - it's something most SEO consultants will check for and there are some great online tools out there you can use to check how original your own content is (try **Copyscape** for one!)

Google is looking for content that is original, timely, relevant and useful.

The same is true when it comes to an SEO strategy.

Someone tell you that they made their fortune by posting adverts on Facebook. Good for them - but that doesn't mean it is going to work for you.

The internet is full of SEO experts, growth hackers, digital marketers, and assorted snake-oil salesmen. I should know.. I've been one of them for over ten years. When someone hits on a technique that works, they tend to share it. Nothing hooks a new client in like a great success story.

The truth is that whilst there are many "evergreen" SEO tactics (and many of them are in this book), you should take any strategy you see a competitor using and consider carefully whether it fits with your strategy or brand before you employ it.

Doing SEO is not like ordering lunch in "When Harry Met Sally" - you can't just "have what she's having".

SEO is not expensive. Low budget? Spend time on creating good content and building relationships online

It doesn't cost a lot of money to do good SEO. In fact, most of the things that you can do as "positive SEO" become worthless, or even negative, for your website if the search engines believe you have bought them.

Example - **paid for back links**.

A back link to your website is generally considered to be a good thing, especially if the website that has linked to yours is authoritative in your particular niche or field.

But, if you have *bought* that backlink its value becomes zero or less.

The very best thing that you can do for your website in terms of SEO is to create great content - something **useful, timely, relevant, and unique**. All it takes is time.

When you've created that content, find somewhere to share it - depending on the audience you want to reach then Facebook, LinkedIn, Medium, or Twitter may be good options for you. With a little luck and a following wind, your content will be found and shared by your target market.

It didn't work - nobody liked my content. You charlatan!

There are lots of reasons this might happen (except the charlatan thing) but, assuming that your content *is* great, I'm going to bet it's **timing**.

For example, the average lifespan of a tweet is **18 minutes**. If nobody has engaged with your tweet after those first 18 minutes, it will have already dropped too far down the majority of users feeds for them to see it. It's easy for your voice to be drowned out on social media, which is why "likes" are so important - content that users engage with gets a longer lifespan, reappears in users feeds, and thus has more chances to engage users.

Social networks thrive on content that engages users - give them what they need and they will support you in return.

#protip: It's OK to re-share your content, just make sure you have enough content so that you are not constantly repeating yourself online.

SEO takes time and results are not instant. Record changes and track what happens to traffic over time

For an industry that is constantly changing, SEO can move *really* slowly sometimes.

Don't expect the search engines to react instantly when you change something - it can take time for spiders (the term for the software that search engines use to "crawl" the web and index sites) to find your new content and add it to the index.

There used to be legends in the SEO industry of search engines putting new domains in a "sandbox" for weeks, even months, before they would hit the index. Google now claim that their RankBrain algorithm can make real-time adjustments.

The reality is that changes **do** take time to affect the overall performance of your website.

SEO, Analytics, and the Butterfly Effect

Let's say we make a change to your website that makes your search engines results better. You move up three whole places, which increases the chances of your result being clicked on by 5%. Would you notice a 5% bump in your traffic or would you ignore it?

Would you notice the 5% bump if, at the same time, a national holiday meant that searches for your the words and phrases you are targeting when down by 4% for the next week?

Big shifts do happen - content can go viral, your brand can hit the news online. But, for the most part, SEO is the art of making multiple changes and improvements, taking multiple steps, each of which will have a small incremental impact on your overall site performance that, over time, do result in a large change.

Butterfly Effect: the phenomenon whereby a minute localized change in a complex system can have large effects elsewhere.

Write everything down

This is why it is incredibly important to keep a track of **what you did** and **when you did it**. We may not notice that our click-throughs have gone up by 5% a week after we make a certain change, but a 5% increase for the entire year is much harder to miss.

The trick is being able to track back to when that improvement began and understanding **why** it happened.

Google Analytics has a great feature that allows you to create an annotation in your analytics, recording something that happened and when.

I encourage all my clients to use annotations to record significant events and changes when they occur so that the causation of a new trend is easy to isolate.

A new domain will take to build up authority. Don't expect to leapfrog older sites overnight

In keeping with the theme of SEO taking time, a word of warning on brand new domains.

Although the legends of "sandboxing" of new sites are no longer true, it **will** take time for your website to build up its authority in your particular vertical or niche.

The good news is that this authority is only important when you are fighting for ranking on keywords and phrases that are already heavily contested and where your competitors have already created good quality content, built links, etc.

The simplest way to make up ground fast to work in areas where your competitors haven't. Just like finding an untapped market, an untapped keyword can be a world of opportunity.

You can use **Google Adwords** to research keywords and find new combinations with low or limited competition. Create content to exploit these areas and ensure you share it - if you create new, great content not only should you attract links but you will also appear in the search engine results for searches that match your new content.

A low authority domain will still rank for keywords where it is a significantly better match than a competitor.

Your SEO project will never, ever be finished. You can always improve. So can your competitors

SEO is an arms race. If you're currently in #1 position for a lucrative search term, chances are the everyone from position #to infinity are gunning for you.

So, it's not just SEO that is changing - it's your competitors.

Maybe you're not number #1 right now. Let's say you're number 4. The difference in click-through rate between the Top 3 organic results and the rest of page one is sharp - you want to be Top 3 if you can't be Number 1. The only way to get one of those coveted top spots, of course, is to **knock someone else out**.

"This ain't a scene, it's a goddamn arms race"
- Fall Out Boy

This is why your SEO project (encompassing all aspects of SEO, SEM, UX etc. as we've talked about) will never be finished. Even if the "rules" of SEO stood still, even if Google finally said "Yep, cracked it, that index is getting no better than it is today" you would still be up against the changes, improvements, and additions your competitors make.

That's why they're called "the competition" and not "people who do the same things as me".

Google is not a black box. Read Webmaster Guidelines and watch Webmaster Help Videos.

SEO is full of contradictions - things that work for other people won't work for you, things that didn't work for other people will propel your sites to heights undreamt of. That's the way the search engines **need** it to be - because if everyone knew exactly how to position a site at #1 in the search engine results, then everyone would do it, #1 position would become worthless and so would the search engines themselves.

Google, in particular, is not as much of a "black box" as it once was. They publish clear guidelines for search, they tweet regular pieces of advice about search engine algorithm changes, and they even share the guidelines that they give their human moderators on how to grade pages.

Wait a minute, did you say human moderators?

Indeed I did. It's not the most widely known thing in the SEO world but Google employs thousands of people worldwide to grade websites and web pages manually. These gradings are fed back into the system and are, in many ways, the raw data from which improvements to the algorithm are formed.

Google wants to give you the "best" answer and has its algorithm tuned to do just that. But was does "best" mean? *That's* why there are human moderators, testing the search index against the criteria that Google have written down for what *they* think makes a page good (or "best").

And, yes, you can get a copy of this document. It's a bit of a beast, 160 pages plus in the latest version I saw, but it is well worth reading - or giving to your web developer and asking them if they've built your site with these in mind.

(Hint: They will probably say "yes", so check yourself. Be your own human moderator.)

The reality of moving between website providers

In my experience, it's rare for one website company to take on the work of another.

Developers *hate* working on what we call "legacy systems" - systems with a history we aren't fully aware of and that we can't be 100% sure is properly documented.

Taking on a website from another developer/agency and providing support on it is like taking on the warranty for a second-hand car that you've never worked on before with no service history and the strong suspicion that that rattling noise under the bonnet is probably something serious.

The reality is that most migrations from one website agency/developer to another involve a rebuild of the website.

This doesn't mean that it is impossible and this is a strength of working with one of the larger Open Source platforms such as Wordpress. There are **lots** of Wordpress developers around getting one to take on your website shouldn't be that hard - just don't be surprised when the suggestion of a rebuild comes along.

Be honest - do these guys just want my money?

In short - yes, of course they do.

The longer answer is that what they want, like any business, is profitable contracts.

Taking on a site built by someone else, even if you understand the technology in detail, always carries a risk. The value of the support contract therefore has to mitigate that risk, or the person taking on the website is potentially going to be losing money.

Replacing the website is therefore more cost effective; a higher project cost but lower ongoing running costs.

Don't freak out when you don't rank for something you didn't optimise for

Sometimes, this happens...

"Hey, SEO guy!"

"Yeah?"

"We don't come up on Google when I search for hats."

"We don't have any pages optimised for hats. We also don't sell hats."

Alright, I *might* be exaggerating for effect, but not by much.

Remember, SEO is weird. You **will** rank for things you don't expect to. You may not rank as well for things you expect to as you want to. You definitely won't rank for things that you don't have on your site.

Think about it - **why the hell would you?**

Google isn't the only game in town. Diversify your traffic sources to be less vulnerable to problems

I've lost count of the number of times I've written the word "Google" while writing this book. Quite a few times, at least, I've written "Google and other search engines" - the SEO author's equivalent of saying "other carbonated beverages are available".

Let's face it - there's no denying Google's dominance in the search engine space. Only one search engine had its name entered into the Oxford English Dictionary as the verb for searching the internet, and it wasn't *Bing*.

Having said that, it may be a small world but it is full to the brim with people... and a lot of them are searching the internet. Just because Bing, Yahoo!, DuckDuckGo, and others hold only a small percentage of the search engine market doesn't mean that they have a small number of users of a small number of searches being run on them.

DuckDuckGo is a great place to go to reach tech-savvy early adopters who value their privacy. Bing is the place to go to talk to people who don't know how to change their default search engine.

There's nothing wrong in my view with checking your search engine ranking on these search engines, and there's definitely nothing wrong with running cost-per-click campaigns on these platforms.

Outside of Google, each other search engine has its own cost per click options available. Competition may be lower in your niche on one of the "other" search engines.

PPC is not SEO but good SEO can reduce the cost of your PPC and make your budget go further

Did you know that the cost of an advert in Google Ads is directly related to how well your web page matches the search terms you're advertising for?

It's true: It's cheaper to advertise against terms your site is optimised for than terms it is not optimised for.

Why does Google do this? Well, my view is that it's part of their approach to ensuring that their index, including their paid for listings, are as egalitarian as possible. By ensuring that websites that are highly relevant to a particular keyword or term can advertise against that keyword/term inexpensively, Google are trying to level the field between small or new businesses and the larger, more established players.

There's also another way of looking at this - *it helps Google too.*

Google sell answers. Forget every other service they offer, every other project they are involved in, their number one cash-cow that underpins the whole thing is **search**.

If every time you went to Google to find something, to *get an answer*, you were inundated with a bunch of irrelevant adverts that took you to websites that weren't relevant to your query, you wouldn't be a happy customer. Maybe, if this happened enough, you wouldn't be a customer at all.

So, by encouraging high relevant sites to advertise, Google is actually improving the quality of the adverts on its site.

Either way, the effect for website owners is that the better your site is optimised for the keywords that you want to advertise for, the better price you will get per click from Google.

That's got to be worth investing some time in.

Have zero tolerance for duplicate content. Eradicate it at every turn

Search engines hate duplicated content. Google, reputedly, has a *"good cop who just watched his partner get gunned down by the local mob boss at his own daughter's wedding when he was just two days off retirement"* level of hatred for duplicate content.

Eliminating duplicates applies to:

1. Page titles
2. Meta titles
3. Meta descriptions
4. Keywords
5. Page content

Think about it this way:

1. Every page on your website must have a singular purpose/topic it addresses.
2. Every page should be the best page on that topic.

If you're able to tick checks 1 and 2 for each and every page on your website, duplication should be at an absolute minimum.

If you have two or more pages that address the same topic - combine them into one, really great, page. Users, and search engines, will love you for it.

Handling duplicate content with canonical tags

Sometimes, eliminating duplicate content is not as easy as we would like it to be.

This is often the case when trying to optimise eCommerce websites where there are multiple versions of the same product, perhaps with only small (but important) differences between them.

Thankfully, there is a technical solution to this problem - the **canonical** tag.

The canonical tag allows you to specify that a given page on a website is not the original (or "canon") version of that page's content and that another page should be indexed in its stead. The benefits of any links pointing to the page should be passed on, in whole or in part, to the page that is the true original ("canonical") version.

Doing this can reduce duplication in the search index and promotes the importance of the original page.

However, a word of caution... the pages that are canonicalised to another page *disappear from the index.*

Canonicalisation Example 1: Good canonicalisation

At widgets.com we used to sell the Widget A1. Now, we've released the Widget B1. There's not a huge difference between A1 and B1.

We want anyone searching for a widget with the properties of Widget B1 to find it, and not to find Widget A1. We suspect A1 is stealing some of B1's thunder, but we don't want to remove it from our website because existing users may want to access some of the documentation etc. for the A1.

By setting the canonical URL of widget A1 to point to widget B1, we make B1 the default page. Any links pointing to the A1 page now pass their link-benefits onto B1 and any search engine index results for A1 will be redirected to B1. However, customers can see still A1 on our website and find it by navigating to it from our homepage.

Canonicalisation Example 1: Bad canonicalisation

At widgets.com we make the Widget C10. We also make the C11, C12, and C13. They are quite similar but there are key differences. Our widgets are well known in the industry (of widgets) and people will often search for them by name (e.g. "Widget C12").

The widgets sell for different prices and our eCommerce platform holds each as its own page. All of the pages are indexed at the moment, but our SEO consultant is telling us we have duplicate content and some of them need to go.

Is this a good case of canonicalisation? **No.**

If we canonicalise C11, C12, and C13 to C10 we would effectively remove these from the search index. Finding them independently would be impossible.

Guest blogging has lost power as an SEO technique but is still great for referral clicks and networking

Guest blogging was, effectively, writing content for other people's websites/blogs in exchange for getting a link in the "author bio" to your website and it was once the darling technique of SEO consultants and content marketers.

Like any technique that becomes popular as a way to improve organic traffic and "game" Google's index, Google quickly made algorithm changes to reduce the value of links generated in this way - guest blogging fell out of vogue as a consequence.

However, just because guest blogging isn't catapulting websites up the search engine rankings like it once did, that doesn't mean that guest blogging is completely valueless.

Guest blogging is the online equivalent to getting the opportunity to speak to someone else's contact list, client base, or customer list. You may share a few contacts but the chances are that the people going to the website that you will be featured on *won't* be people who know you, your products, your work, or your website.

Whilst Google may have devalued the power of this endorsement as a pure link-building strategy, having your content featured on bigger sites with a wider audience than your own is still a powerful way to build your brands platform.

It's not all about rank. Ranking 1st for a keyword that generates no sales is pointless.

I decided to leave this until the very end of the book as ranking websites for useless "junk terms" is **literally the oldest trick in the SEO book.**

I can definitely, 100%, without question get any website to the number one position on Google - **if I get to choose the keyword**.

Don't fall for it.

The purpose of your website is not to be no.1 on a search engine. It's to generate as much return on investment as possible.

Working with SEO Consultants and Agencies

I wrote this book mostly because I was tired of finding my industry down on the same list as bankers, double glazing sales, estate agents, and dentists.

I'd want to reach the pearly gates just to discover that Dante had been brought out of retirement to craft a special new level of hell just for website developers, digital marketers, and IT consultants.

Not all companies selling SEO, CPC, digital marketing, and the like are bad. Sadly, quite a few **are** and whilst there are more businesses that need these services than people providing them, "bad apples" are getting a free ride, able to move when they need to - leaving chaos and carnage in their wake.

Hopefully, this book leaves you more empowered to tell the bad from the good, make your own way online, and use consultants and third parties in the right way - **where we add value**.

Nothing makes a good consultant happier in their work than when **it works**.

Don't be afraid to ask consultants lots of questions. They should be asking you lots of questions because, unless they've worked in your industry and with your business before, there's always a lot to learn.

Never trust a consultant who keeps their techniques a secret. We're not wizards, we're mostly just looking things up on Google just like the rest of you.

Last but not least...

Well, that's it. More than a decade of lessons, insights, and probably too many film quotes. I hope it helps you with your business, whatever it may be.

Before I go, here's one final thought...

No matter you do to your website, **do it for your customer.**

I wholeheartedly believe that a website built for the customer first, the customer second, the customer third, and the customer last will be a website that grows, thrives, and can survive the crazy rollercoaster run by crocodiles with lasers for eyes that is the digital world right now.

Good luck, and thanks for reading.

OK, so that was not quite the last...

Was there something that didn't make sense? Something you still really need to know?

Try checking out my business website https://www.gravite.co.uk or find us on Twitter @**gravitetech**

Ask us a question - we don't bite and I love a good puzzle.

Printed in Great Britain
by Amazon